INSTANT

ENGLISH
LITERATURE

INSTANT

ENGLISH

LITERATURE

THE NINETEENTH CENTURY

BY ROSEMARY GELSHENEN

A Byron Preiss Book

FAWCETT COLUMBINE • NEW YORK

CONTENTS

INTRODUCTION

It's Friday night and you're in the mood for a *real* book. Your soul is crying out for a novel with *meaning*. You've read too many potboilers lately—books whose heroines do nothing but toss their hair and throw sultry looks at tightly clothed buccaneers named Lance. It's time for a book with some meat on its bones.

So you head down to the local bookstore and scan the classics section. What should you buy? To make sure you cover all the bases, you pick out an armload of titles you dimly recall from English Literature 101. Two months later the books remain where you left them, unread. The dust on the stack is pretty impressive. Time passes. A lot of time. You know it's all over when you buy a mystery novel featuring Colt Python as the main character. You feel cheap in the morning.

Or, maybe you have an exam three days from now for a survey course called something like: Recursive Diacritical Trends In The Nineteenth-Century British Novel. Alas, the professor has assigned a few dozen tomes, which *you've* assigned to a bottom shelf in your dorm room, until finals roar toward you like a train in the night.

WE CAN TELL: *INSTANT ENGLISH LITERATURE* IS FOR YOU

In this survey of the best novels of nineteenth-century England, you'll learn how the works of fourteen famous authors fit into literary history's big picture. You'll get a list of each author's best-known works, a concise biography, and a critical analysis of the author's professional career. Easy-to-understand analysis reveals the literary trends these writers established—or ignored. Finally, a variety of lighthearted sidebars will distract you from weightier topics like theme, character, plot, context, and, one hopes, little-known naughty habits. You will come away full of inside knowledge about the hidden allusions and unexpected connections that give great works of literature their full-bodied flavor.

THE VICTORIAN AGE, OR, "THEY WERE SO MODEST, EVEN THE TABLE LEGS WORE PANTS."

Mid-nineteenth-century England is often referred to as the Victorian Age after a stout, stern-faced queen—think of the transvestite movie star Divine, in a tiara—whose reign extended for some sixty-four years. Queen Victoria left her mark on all aspects of British society, including its literature. Before Victoria's reign, Jane Austen poked fun at provincial manners, and later Anthony Trollope and William Makepeace Thackeray followed suit with some of the funniest satires in literature. After Victoria ascended the throne, literature would subtly evolve, partly in response to the character of her rule.

Victoria (1819–1901, reigned 1837–1901) was no figurehead. She didn't merely appear for a ribbon cutting at the pickle works or pretend to admire cheesy lamps manufactured in her likeness. Victoria actually ruled, making all the great decisions of state, and extended England's empire, in the words of Rudyard Kipling, "from palm to pine"—that is, "from pole to pole." In Victoria's time, England governed large slices of the world: India, Ireland, South Africa, Australia, Canada, and lots of islands. Hers was a period of intense patriotism, rigid public morality, and great literature. Soldiers and sailors willingly died for Queen and country. Home and family were revered and marriage was a serious business. The Queen's life with her consort, Albert, was by all accounts quite happy. But it would be wrong to assume that such bliss led to a relaxed attitude in the realm of domestic affairs. The Queen imposed on her subjects such a rigid morality that even today the word Victorian connotes repressed sexuality. In those days, anything a missionary wouldn't do had to be done in the closet.

During Victoria's reign, writers and their texts evolved along with concurrent trends in British society. In that era, people preached on behalf of what was morally acceptable, but often practiced modes of behavior that were anything but pure. Charles Dickens' heroes led irreproachable lives, but Dickens himself carried on a secret, adulterous affair with a woman young enough to be his daughter. Though the female writer George Eliot (they published under men's names in those days) resided with her lover "without benefit of clergy," she dutifully punished in fiction those characters who strayed from the path of righteousness.

As the nineteenth century's "Industrial Revolution" gathered steam, British society became afflicted with a variety of urban ills. Thus child labor, debtors' prison, sweatshops, hunger, disease, and illiteracy became key themes in a new type of literature, the novel of social reform. "Man's inhumanity to man" had already become a topic of interest, hence the plight of Mary Shelley's pathetic monster in the novel *Frankenstein*. But it was Charles Dickens who awakened British readers to the real-life tragedy of poverty and oppression. Dickens became a champion of orphans and waifs while amusing his readers with unforgettable caricatures of rogues, villains, and the merely eccentric. George Eliot, meanwhile, exposed the caste system in country life, from the lonely weaver to the betrayed milkmaid. A true nineteenth-century feminist, she consistently gave the reader heroines who were often smarter than their mates. The Brontë sisters, writing in the obscurity of the Yorkshire moors, used their own real-life experiences to illustrate the lousy lot of the lowly governess. Despite the multitude of hardships that beset such characters, optimism prevailed. Readers expected and usually got happy endings.

With the remarkable growth of the British Empire, the novel gained new dimensions. By midcentury, England was no longer defined by its island borders. Travelers and soldiers brought back fascinating tales of the newly discovered "dark continent" and of the mysterious East Indies. Joseph Conrad, who began his career as a sailor, and Rudyard Kipling, a reporter, returned from little-known climes with tales of distant adventure. Other English adventurers, like Robert Louis Stevenson, spun romantic stories of the South Sea islands, stories brimming with buccaneers and pirates (none of them named Lance).

When Queen Victoria died at the age of 82, so did the air of fantasy and adventure that had imbued the work of writers active during the latter part of her reign. Even before she died, Thomas Hardy was reminding his readers in brutal fashion that "all romance ends in marriage." In short, fatalism became the vogue. Try as they might to escape their destiny, the heroines of Thomas Hardy and Henry James were created by writers determined to weave unsentimental endings. Such authors displayed a new kind of realism, in which characters did not (or could not) conform to the idealized norms of polite society. Instead they possessed virtues and flaws like the rest of us, making them more credible representatives of real life.

Still, in real life, the greatest works of literature can seem distant if not plain intimidating. Like that amusing friend who aced every Lit course he or she ever took, this book chases meaning and lets *you* cut to enjoyment.

ENGLISH
LITERATURE

CHAPTER 1

JANE AUSTEN
(1775–1817)

YOU MUST REMEMBER THIS

Jane Austen gave the English novel its modern form, forsaking the trite, moralistic themes of her predecessors and developing instead the rich characterizations and stylistic control for which she is still renowned. Her favorite subject: how to get your man.

MOST FAMOUS FOR

- ★ *Sense and Sensibility* (1811)
- ★ *Pride and Prejudice* (1813)
- ★ *Mansfield Park* (1814)
- ★ *Emma* (1816)
- ★ *Northanger Abbey* (1818)
- ★ *Persuasion* (1818)

"**O**h! it is only a novel!" exclaims a character in Austen's *Northanger Abbey* "... or, in short, only some work in which the most thorough knowledge of human nature, the happiest delineation of its varieties, the liveliest effusions of wit and humor are to be conveyed to the world in the best-chosen language." It is a creed that all modern novelists (down to our own Sidney Sheldon) have tried to live up to, but none perhaps as successfully as Jane Austen. The richness and variety of her work have earned her the title, "the Shakespeare of novelists."

SENSE AND NONSENSE

AUSTEN MEETS SARTRE

Sunday morning service in Austen's England.

THE LIFE AND TIMES OF MISS JANE AUSTEN

The sixth of seven children of a country parson, Jane Austen was born at Steventon in Hampshire, which she immortalized in her sketches of provincial society. She grew up with family parties and picnics, home theatricals, country dances, and most importantly, a good-sized library where the impressionable young girl enjoyed both serious literature and very bad novels.

Though most of her novels are about the machinations that matchmaking and husband-hunting set in motion, Austen never married, though she did temporarily accept a proposal from the aptly named Harris Bigg-Wither (his suit withered in a big way). The engagement lasted less than a day. After a sleepless night, it was Austen who withered, and told her swain she couldn't go through with the marriage. Her family was doubtlessly dismayed to see such an opportunity gained and lost all in one day, even if this fine prospect was six years her junior, and seemed to have the intellectual brio of a plate of kippers.

Austen died on July 18, 1817, and was buried in the cathedral at Winchester. Her bankrupt—financially, not morally—brother Henry oversaw publication of her last two novels, *Northanger Abbey* and *Persuasion*.

To the contemporary reader, what may seem odder than Austen's decision not to marry is how avidly she avoided the "literary life." She sought neither the security nor the instant approval that affiliation with a particular literary school or movement brings a writer. It was her unflagging devotion to the craft of novel-writing that earned her the respect of her literary peers—including Coleridge, Southey, and Mme. de Staël. And so it is appropriate that we put aside the circumstances of her life, and focus on Austen's works.

BEST-KNOWN NOVEL

Pride and Prejudice

"It is a truth universally acknowledged that a single man in possession of a good fortune must be in want of a wife." This is the famous opening sentence from *Pride and Prejudice*, a sentence in which Austen both sets the narrative in motion and establishes the narrator's ironic tone. Not only does the word *must* announce the marital imperative that shapes her novels, it is also a good example of the slyly humorous outlook for which she is justly renowned.

A writer less attentive to the nuances of speech than Austen might have contented herself with merely "a single man *is* in want of a wife." But in this detail she sums up the assumption of the mothers and daughters who came into contact with such a man. He *must* want a wife because we want him to marry us or one of our female dependents, as the case may be. Thus, the opening sentence contains a clue to the provincial views that existed in the time and place where the novel is set: a small town in nineteenth-century England. Through the deadpan earnestness with which Austen presented the petty tensions of genteel domestic life, she achieved a fresh amusing effect. She transformed the novel of manners into the comedy of manners.

Welcome to Meryton, a town perhaps much like Austen's own hometown of Steventon. As the novel opens, Mrs. Bennet, the looming maternal presence, informs Mr. Bennet that Netherfield Park has been let to a wealthy young man, Mr. Bingley, whose income is roughly £5000 a year. Mind you, in those days, a gentleman did not work. Money properly came in the form of income from one's inheritance or rent from one's property.

Mrs. Bennet, Austen writes, "was a woman of mean understanding, little information, and uncertain temper. The business of her life was to get her daughters married; its solace was visiting and news." At the beginning of the novel, Mrs. Bennet's sights are already set on Mr. Bingley as a possible match for one of her daughters.

WHO'S
H O 👉

Pride and Prejudice:
A LITERARY TOUT SHEET

Mrs. Bennet: Mother of five daughters whom she is trying desperately to marry off.

Mr. Bennet: Her absent-minded husband, who avoids family problems by retreating to his library.

The Bennet sisters:
  Jane, the eldest, falls in love with Charles Bingley.
  Elizabeth, Jane Austen's heroine, spirited and independent, a good match for the haughty Fitzwilliam Darcy.
  Lydia, the youngest, foolish and an easy mark for a cad like George Wickham.

Charles Bingley: Falls in love with Jane Bennet but is easily talked out of it by his snobbish sisters and his friend Darcy.

Fitzwilliam Darcy: Wealthier even than Bingley and far more eligible. At first a snob, he is finally conquered by Elizabeth.

Lady Catherine: Darcy's haughty aunt, worse than a mother-in-law.

George Wickham: An impoverished army officer and a womanizer—a real cad.

There is a reason for Mrs. Bennet's overbearing efforts on her daughters' behalf. When her husband came into his inheritance, the will stipulated that if he lacked a male heir of his own, his wealth and estate would pass to his closest male relative, an unctuous toad of a clergyman named Collins. The girls are to lose everything upon their father's death. For good girls like the Bennets there were just a few vocational choices in such a situation: to become teachers, governesses, or wives.

There are five Bennet girls, all "in want of a hus-

George IV (1762–1830).
His extravagance as bad-boy
Prince Regent set the tone
for the Regency period.

REGENCY ENGLAND

The Regency period is a term most commonly used to refer to the styles, especially in fashion and furniture, found in England during the regency of George, Prince of Wales. His father, George III, who lost England's American colonies, had gone permanently insane, and while waiting to come of age, George IV was known as the Prince Regent. His regency lasted from 1811 to 1820, when he ascended to the throne as George IV and ruled England until 1830.

band"—Jane, Elizabeth, Mary, Kitty, and Lydia; in accordance with the etiquette of Regency England, Jane as the eldest ought to be the first one to marry and thus pave the way for her sisters. Wouldn't Mr. Bingley be just perfect for Jane? In fact, he is. Jane and Charles Bingley meet at a ball, where they dance twice and hit it off exceedingly well.

Also at the ball, in Bingley's company, are his sister Caroline and a Mr. Fitzwilliam Darcy. Imagine yourself as James Bond with the wealth of J. P. Morgan. Might such good fortune lead to overconfidence or maybe even

THE NOVEL OF MANNERS AND THE ENLIGHTENMENT

Henry Fielding (1707–1754).

Jane Austen's novels were published just a few decades after the eighteenth century's most significant innovation in English prose fiction: the Novel of Manners. The most accomplished example in this genre is Henry Fielding's *Tom Jones* (a book that has nothing to do with the randy Welsh singer of the same name). The Novel of Manners deals in human types, rather than the kind of nuanced characterizations Jane Austen creates.

The Novel of Manners is characteristic of the Age of Enlightenment, a period in eighteenth-century European intellectual history when writers and thinkers were committed to the pursuit of grand abstract truths (like Liberty, Equality, Fraternity), and human progress. In short, Enlightenment thinkers believed man was perfectible. A arrogance? That's Mr. Darcy—accomplished, handsome, haughty, and blessed with an annuity of £10,000 a year.

Jane is invited to visit the Bingleys and ends up staying longer than anyone expected. She has caught a cold on her way to Netherfield so the Bingleys feel obliged to nurse her back to health (try this yourself sometime when you're visiting a friend and when the notion of staying on a few weeks is broached you'll see how times have changed).

When Jane's not busy insinuating herself into the affections of Mr. Bingley, she's entertaining her family,

group of eighteenth-century writers as varied as Henry Fielding, Daniel Defoe, and Samuel Richardson displayed at least some desire to offer moral instruction. Their heroes and heroines (for instance, Clarissa in Samuel Richardson's novel of that name) rarely act—they are acted upon. Clarissa says what she means; she is never indirect, she never equivocates, and her personality never evolves. In his mission to instruct the reader, the novelist of manners uses such a heroine like a buoy to mark off various abstract qualities found in society: charity, lust, cruelty, piety, etc. Moral flaws are embodied in the evil characters that revolve around the Novel of Manners' heroine.

Liberté, Égalité, Fraternité—*sounds even grander and more abstract in French,* non?

especially Elizabeth, who regularly comes to visit during her convalescence. Jane's illness might be termed the shrewdest malady in the history of literature because while Elizabeth is attending Jane, Darcy becomes rather fond of the younger sister. He enjoys her wit and energy, qualities missing from the other female company of Darcy's world.

While Mr. Darcy is warming to Lizzy's charms, the noxious Mr. Collins comes to visit with a fine idea that since he is Mr. Bennet's heir he will make what amends he can to the Bennet family by marrying one of the girls. Jane? No, she's virtually engaged. Lizzy? She'll do. Unfortunately for Collins, he will not do from Lizzy's point of view. His proposal is rejected. Collins has more success with Charlotte Lucas, a very poor friend of the Bennet girls who needs the money badly enough to marry him.

In the meantime, Lizzy has been advised by George Wickham that Darcy is not merely arrogant but dishonorable as well. Wickham should know; as boys he and Darcy were raised together by Darcy's father. Wickham implies that Darcy violated the father's will and cheated Wickham out of some money. When Lizzy asks Darcy for an explanation, Darcy demurs, saying his sense of honor prevents him from discussing the matter.

And what's the explanation for the Bingleys' subsequent departure for London? Jane understands it to signify a rejection, and she's right. Lizzy tries to solace her by suggesting that Bingley hasn't changed his heart, merely his address.

When Darcy encounters Lizzy again, he confesses that he loves her and then condescendingly demands her hand in marriage. But this vain man, ever-conscious of his high social status, bungles his chances by offering one of the most conceited proposals any suitor has ever inflicted upon a woman. The spirited Lizzy flatly refuses him.

In the meantime, George Wickham has run off with young Lydia Bennet (in Meryton, that's how you spell *scandal*). Eventually, Wickham agrees to marry the girl for a dowry that even Mr. Bennet considers to be a reasonable sum. Why? Darcy himself has set up Wickham with a large "allowance" in order to alleviate the Bennet family's moral quandary and financial burdens. Wickham, it turns out, had once tried the same stunt with Darcy's sister and ruined her reputation.

Ah-ha! This is why honor prohibited Mr. Darcy from badmouthing that cad, Elizabeth now realizes. To tell the truth would be to implicate his sister in a foul deed from the past. Both Darcy's explanation and his benevolence have turned Lizzy's heart toward Darcy once again. Of course, it doesn't hurt that this time around Darcy steps off his marble pedestal long enough to propose marriage again, with at least a tinge of humility and sufficient ardor to gain Lizzy's assent. Bingley and Jane are soon reconciled, and they marry too.

AUSTEN VERSUS THE NOVEL OF MANNERS

A novelist of manners might have made the eldest sister, Jane Bennet, the heroine of *Pride and Prejudice*. After all, she is beautiful, somewhat accomplished, dreamy, and most of all, easily knocked down by the savage seas of upper-crust social life. But instead, Elizabeth is the central character of this novel.

In many ways, her character broke new ground. Though not a commoner, she wasn't the usual highborn lady of contemporary fiction. She was independent enough to reject a first proposal from a rich, socially superior gentleman. Her own personality was not unrelievedly pure as the driven snow. And most important, Elizabeth gained new understanding of herself and her world over the course of the book. She matured.

Jane Austen, who was more interested in art than instruction, broke new ground by showing us a fictional society that was not made lifeless by a heavy load of good and evil symbolism. She held a more truly reflective mirror up to life. Paradoxically, readers learn more from Austen about how society actually works than we do from a novelist of manners, whose pat distillations of human nature lack the ring of truth. Jane Austen stepped away from the routine characterizations to which her predecessors adhered by endowing her characters with realistic assets and imperfections. She exposed the snobbery and hypocrisy that she witnessed every day in her small social circle. It has been said that when she attended parties she had a notebook discreetly secreted in her dress. Between this habit of social spying and the prevailing prejudices against female authorship in her day, it's no wonder her first novels were published under the pseudonym "A Lady." Austen was indeed a pioneer, which is why she's often thought of as the first modern novelist.

WHO'S WHO

Mansfield Park:
A LITERARY TOUT SHEET

Sir Thomas and Lady Bertram: Wealthy, socially-minded owners of Mansfield Park and parents of two daughters, Maria and Julia, and two sons, Tom and Edmund.

Maria Bertram: Engaged to one man but attracted to another. She and her sister Julia, as well as their brother Tom, treat the heroine, Fanny Price, with contempt because she is poor.

Edmund Bertram: The only Bertram who is not a snob. He befriends his cousin, Fanny Price, and eventually marries her.

Fanny Price: The heroine of the story and the poor relation of the Bertrams.

Henry Crawford: Neighbor to the Bertrams. He runs off with Maria Bertram after she marries another man, James Rushworth.

Mary Crawford: Henry's sister. Edmund Bertram thinks he is in love with her, but she turns him down because he is a clergyman (and she's looking for bigger fish).

TWO OTHER NOVELS
BRIEFLY DISCUSSED

Mansfield Park

Lizzy Bennet is loved by Darcy for the same reason she's at the center of *Pride and Prejudice:* her wit and intellectual energy. Even her creator couldn't help but love her. Austen once wrote in a letter: "I must confess that I think her as delightful a creature as ever appeared in print, and how I shall be able to tolerate those who do not like *her* at least I do not know. . . ." It's fair enough that as readers we not only tend to side with the author's most likable characters, we also associate that character with the author herself. And yet Austen played against that easy expectation.

In *Mansfield Park*, published the year after *Pride and Prejudice,* Mary Crawford is much like Lizzy Bennet—lively, open, intelligent, attractive to and attracted by men. But Mary isn't at all likable. Neither, at first, is Fanny Price, the focus of this book. Fanny's a poor girl who goes to live with wealthier relatives, and for obvious reasons their relations are a bit strained. She's a nice girl, perhaps too nice, but by the end you come to appreciate Fanny's real virtues. Austen's fans considered the book a flop at the time, but what saves it is the fact that again Austen refuses to deal in stereotypes—the novel's a realistic portrayal of specific characters.

Emma

If you think Mary Crawford isn't likable, wait until you meet Emma Woodhouse! A meddlesome snob, Emma is determined to interfere in other people's lives. When she successfully marries off her former governess, Emma boasts: "You cannot think I shall leave off matchmaking." She tries to engineer a match between her protégée, the seventeen-year-old Harriet Smith, and the young

WHO'S HO ☞

Emma:
A LITERARY TOUT SHEET

Mr. Woodhouse: Widowed father of Emma, a real hypochondriac who hates change.

Emma Woodhouse: His daughter, who finally learns her lesson and stops matchmaking.

Harriet Smith: Emma's protégée, who really loves the farmer Robert Martin, until Emma talks her out of it.

Mr. Elton: A young clergyman, a victim of Emma's matchmaking.

Frank Churchill: A man about town. Emma thinks she might match him with Harriet, but he is already engaged to Jane Fairfax.

Jane Fairfax: Poor but attractive young woman who is loved by Frank Churchill. Emma is somewhat jealous of her.

George Knightley: A friend of the Woodhouse family. He disapproves of Emma's matchmaking, but falls in love with her nevertheless.

vicar, Mr. Elton. Meanwhile, she breaks up Harriet's romance with Robert Martin, whom she dubs "a very inferior creature" because he is a farmer.

Emma gets her comeuppance when Harriet schemes to win the very eligible George Knightley, whom Emma realizes—almost too late—that she herself loves. All ends happily when the chastened heroine gives up matchmaking to plan her own wedding to Mr. Knightley.

Many critics consider *Emma* to be Austen's structural masterpiece. Consider the skillful manipulation it takes to get your readers to root for a heroine who most often deserves a good swift kick!

A Closing Word

Austen wrested the novel from the eighteenth-century notion that morality was something abstract and external. She suggested that morals are not dictated by a higher authority, but are formed by people as they interact with each other. The duty of an author is not to moralize, but to portray human actions and emotions as they actually occur. This belief fit neatly with her desire to satirize the middle class.

SUMMARY

- Invigorated the novel by bringing psychological depth to her characterizations.

- Satirized provincial middle-class values.

- Exposed small-town snobbery and hypocrisy.

- Never married, though that institution was a central theme of her work.

CHAPTER 2

THE BRONTËS

ANNE BRONTË
(1820–1849)
CHARLOTTE BRONTË
(1816–1855)
EMILY BRONTË
(1818–1848)

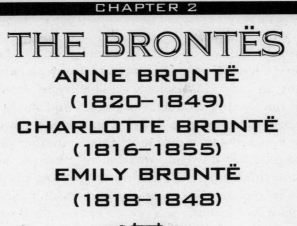

YOU MUST REMEMBER THIS

A family almost as talented as the Marxes, the Brontës produced three world-famous novelists. The "Zeppo Marx" of the clan was brother Branwell, a dipsomaniacal artist.

MOST FAMOUS FOR

Anne: ★ *Agnes Grey* (1847)
             ★ *The Tenant of Wildfell Hall* (1848)
Charlotte: ★ *Jane Eyre* (1847)
             ★ *Shirley* (1849)
             ★ *Villette* (1853)
             ★ *The Professor* (1857, published posthumously)
Emily: ★ *Wuthering Heights* (1847)

Isn't it odd that one family should produce three so very talented writers? Actually, as anyone who was not an only child knows, sibling rivalry frequently brings out the best as well as the worst; and the best way to beat your brothers or sisters is to defeat them utterly in the endeavors they care most about. Another possible explanation for this concentration of talent is that the isolation the Brontë sisters endured growing up on the moors forced them to count on one another for entertainment. As Nintendo was not an option, they made up stories and even collaborated on an early book of verse, the *Gondal* poems. Gondal was a mythical land dominated by cruel, ruthless people—much like the real world. Unfortunately the book sold only two copies—a publishing record that may still stand.

PSEUDONYMS . . . .

The Brontës, like many other English women who published in the nineteenth century, disguised their true identities. It was considered improper in these days for a lady to express herself in print, especially in the emotionally intimate manner that fiction requires. But rather than adopting masculine names, they published under the androgynous pseudonyms Acton Bell (Anne), Currer Bell (Charlotte), and Ellis Bell (Emily).

THE STORY OF A MAN NAMED BRONTË

By modern standards, the formative years of the Brontë sisters were marked by the kind of deprivation

*The Reverend
Patrick Brontë.*

that could make a chain gang seem inviting, if only for the chance to sing along with others. Their father was the Reverend Patrick Brontë, who once burned his children's new red shoes because they were "too gay and luxurious," and cut his wife's favorite silk dress to shreds. Had he learned to relax when it came to hip threads, his offspring might have contented themselves with more modest amusements. In short, the Brontës weren't so much driven as they were goaded to imaginative escape. Their curate father was himself an author, one who encouraged his children to read. Today we would characterize their home as one where animated political discussions were common and animated cartoons were not.

The Brontë household was always just one step ahead of the bill collector, but many steps behind the Joneses. As a result of their poverty, Charlotte and Anne were forced to work as governesses. Charlotte once remarked to Elizabeth Gaskell that "only those who had been in the position of governess could realize the dark side of 'respectable' human nature." And yet as writers are wont to use their life for their work, both Brontës drew on their experiences to create governess heroines, Charlotte in *Jane Eyre* and Anne in *Agnes Grey*.

To solve the family's deepening money crisis, Patrick Brontë decided to open a school, and sent Charlotte and Emily off to Brussels, so they could learn enough about foreign languages to teach at the new school.

In Brussels, Charlotte fell in love with the charming

ELIZABETH CLEGHORN GASKELL (1810–1865)

A friend and contemporary of the Brontës, she was a popular novelist who often wrote in Charles Dickens' magazines *Household Words* and *All the Year Round.* Gaskell is best known for her controversial views of social problems, such as her criticism of industrial abuses in *Mary Barton.* Her biography of Charlotte Brontë, published in 1857, caused a sensation at the time, and she was forced by relatives of the Brontës to publicly retract parts of it—no doubt, the more interesting parts.

Constantin Héger, who became the model for her later romantic heroes, including Edward Rochester in *Jane Eyre.* After less than a year, the Brontë sisters returned to England. Although their school never opened, by 1847 all three Brontë sisters had written novels, one of which—Charlotte's *Jane Eyre*—was an instant success.

It can be hard to keep track of the authors and their various titles. Here's how to tell them apart:

Charlotte (1816–55) was the most prolific. In her most famous work, *Jane Eyre*, the author created an autobiographical novel that broke with tradition. Instead of employing the contrived sentimentality found in the heroines of lesser writers, Charlotte invented a passionate, underprivileged young woman whose powerful longings caused a sensation. And she was the first novelist to give us a heroine who was not beautiful. (The expression "a plain Jane," referring to a rather unattractive female, is taken from Brontë's description of her main character.)

Emily (1818–48) was the most enigmatic sister. We have limited direct information about her, but can deduce from the stormy lives portrayed in *Wuthering Heights* that the author's reticent personality caged a cauldron of intense feelings. Or maybe she really was dull and the spirits of Heathcliff and Cathy told her what to write.

Anne (1820–1849) may not have had Charlotte's talent for showing the animal impulse at the base of real love, nor Emily's predilection for tempestuous tragedy. But she did follow an urge, unusual in those days, to portray the unpleasant side of existence alongside the good. Her depiction of an alcoholic in *The Tenant of Wildfell Hall* shocked her sister Charlotte, who knew that the characterization was based on their dissolute brother Branwell.

THE POVERTY OF THE CLERGY

We refer here both to the spiritual poverty of the higher church officials, and the actual dire financial straits in which lower officials found themselves. In the Anglican Church of the nineteenth century, bishops and other high-ranking clergymen received enormous salaries, while the lower church officials—those who actually came into contact with parishioners—received almost nothing. Since employment under God was based on political influence, it was not unusual for wealthy churchmen never to visit their parishes at all, and instead to cultivate their contacts in fashionable London or Paris while paying someone else to perform their duties. Actually, a similar hierarchy can be found in many universities, where graduate students do the teaching and full professors take sabbaticals in sunny Italy or some other hardship post.

Nineteenth-century Brussels certainly left its mark on the imaginations and the writings of Charlotte and Emily Brontë. (It was bound to—they generally didn't get out much.) Charlotte based her final work, Villette, *on her experiences at a Belgian boarding school.*

CHARLOTTE'S BEST-KNOWN NOVEL

Jane Eyre

Until the age of ten, the orphaned Jane Eyre is raised by her uncaring aunt, Mrs. Reed. Relations between Jane and the Reed household, which includes a cruel son named John and a vapid budding fashion plate called Georgiana, become unbearably strained. Jane, the unwanted waif, is sent away to Lowood, a fanatically strict Christian boarding school. The harsh living conditions at boarding school and the unduly confining atmo-

Charlotte Brontë (1816–1855). Big sister to English Lit's most famous clan, published under the pseudonym Currer Bell.

sphere of Lowood were based on real life, as was the epidemic that fells a number of the girl inmates of the fictitious institution. While enrolled in a similarly harsh boarding school, the two elder Brontë sisters, Maria and Elizabeth, died in 1825. At the fictional Lowood, the food was "served in two huge tin-plated vessels whence rose a strong steam redolent of rancid fat." (The English, who are not normally known for their culinary expertise, actually do a rather delicate and tasty little dessert with rancid fat.)

Jane distinguishes herself as a superior student and even teaches at Lowood before leaving to take a job as governess at Thornfield, a splendid country estate. Jane's mission is to instruct the master's foster child. She soon comes to enjoy the child's company, and to savor the improvement in basic comfort that her employment brings. But mere freedom from want loses its charm after a while. Yet Jane doesn't have to parry boredom for long. She finally gets to meet Edward Fairfax Rochester. The lord of the manor is a man in his late thirties who, though not handsome, possesses nonetheless an attractive animalistic energy. Jane realizes that she's fallen in love with her boss after the first of several mysterious scenes: One night, Jane sees smoke coming from the master's room and douses his blazing bed with water, saving his life. Rochester bids her not to mention the incident to anyone, and implies that one of the servants, Grace Poole, is at fault. Gradually, Jane and the reader begin to suspect that there's a lunatic presence in the house.

After engaging in desultory courtship with a beautiful rural aristocrat, Miss Ingram, Rochester finally comes around and proposes to Jane. On the big day, it is revealed that Rochester is already married—and indeed he is, to the totally mad Bertha Mason Rochester, a violent psychotic kept locked upstairs. Jane flees Thornfield but, lacking funds, she is soon reduced to begging. She collapses one rainy night, only to be rescued by a clergyman, St. John Rivers (pronounce his first name the way the English do: sin jin), who will turn out to be a distant relation.

St. John and his two sweet sisters take Jane in, and in time she's like part of the family. But as men will, St. John spoils everything. He first makes trouble by asking Jane to study an obscure Asian language. Jane can't imagine why this cold fish in clerical robes is trying to teach her Hindustani but, what the heck, he's been a good host and so she complies. Then his perversely unromantic reasoning is revealed. He wants her to know how to order samosas like a native when they reach their new home, as a married missionary couple, in India! Jane considers the position, but is not thus inclined.

She abandons Rivers when she has a dream that Rochester needs her, and returns to Thornfield only to find that it has become a hollow and burnt-out shell. Jane learns that Rochester's insane wife torched the place, causing her own death. Rochester was crippled and blinded in the process. When Jane finds Rochester, she convinces the self-pitying man that she still carries a

FORESHADOWING

Foreshadowing is a dramatic and novelistic technique used to prepare a reader or audience for future events. The Russian dramatist and short-story writer Anton Chekhov advised writers that, if they use a gun as a prop in their plays, that gun had better go off by the end. Gloomy lighting in a play, or eerie music in a film, or mysterious incidents in a novel, can increase dramatic suspense by leading the audience of a work of art to anticipate strange events. In *Jane Eyre*, by way of a series of inexplicable events, the author foreshadows a terrible secret, namely, the crazy wife whom Rochester keeps in his attic.

torch for him, as it were, so he proposes again. She accepts. Little Jane is happy at last, especially when Rochester regains much of his sight after the birth of their child.

JANE AIRS HER OWN VIEWS

Jane Eyre is a first-person narrative. It's not an autobiography, but an autobiographical novel. The latter literary form was comparatively rare in the early 1800s. Jane is a physically unremarkable young woman, like Charlotte herself. Unlike Austen's Lizzy Bennet, Jane seldom sparkles. It takes some time before her classmates—or Rochester—come to recognize her subtle virtues, what Rochester calls the "savage beautiful creature" that defines Jane's fundamental nature.

What Charlotte Brontë depicts in *Jane Eyre* is a version of romantic love that is not confined to physically or even socially attractive people. This kind of real love could happen to anyone. Jane Eyre is not a dramatic heroine like one of Sir Walter Scott's ethereal and languishing brides. And the enigmatic Rochester is modeled after Contantin Héger, the married Belgian professor with whom Charlotte fell hopelessly in love. By accurately portraying the desires of common people (meaning that anyone, not just a Celtic princess or an aristocrat, is capable of a profound love), Charlotte Brontë did for the English novel what Wordsworth had done for English poetry.

Like Wordsworth, although she uses her own self as the source of her art, what makes her work accessible to us is her sympathetic imagination, her ability to conceive of a life other than her own. On the other hand, to find a writer who turns farther inward toward the self and its desires, we turn no farther than Charlotte's sister Emily.

EMILY'S BEST-KNOWN NOVEL

*Emily Brontë
(1818–1848).*

Wuthering Heights

"Wuther" means roar or bluster, a fair description of what happens on the moors, where this eerie novel is set. And Wuthering Heights is where our narrator, a Mr. Lockwood, comes to meet his new landlord, Mr. Heathcliff. One night, while Lockwood is visiting, the weather becomes so bad that he asks to stay for the night. Heathcliff reluctantly assents. Lockwood wakes in the middle of the night from a terrible dream and, reaching for the window, grasps instead a cold hand—and it talks! Yow! Lockwood merely screams! Most of us would have reached for a chainsaw. Heathcliff bursts in and Lockwood leaves, for by this time he would brave a cyclone to get back home to Thrushcross Grange. Safely ensconced and slightly drier, Lockwood asks his housekeeper, Nelly Dean, to explain.

Wuthering Heights was once the happy home of the Earnshaws, she relates, happy, that is, until the well-meaning master of the house brought home a swarthy young waif named Heathcliff. In this manner the entire story is recounted, with occasional breaks in which Lockwood and Dean reflect on the strange tale as it unfolds. Lockwood had to have sufficient fortitude—and maybe a hollow leg—to endure such a lengthy narrative over a cuppa tea, but such were the narrative "framing" devices of nineteenth-century fiction.

The story: The master's young son Hindley is jealous of this new rival for his father's affections. Meanwhile, Earnshaw's daughter Catherine loves Heathcliff. Once Mr. Earnshaw dies, Hindley takes charge, and uses Heathcliff like a servant. Of course, part of Hindley's motivation is to degrade Heathcliff so thoroughly that Cathy will find it impossible to love him. It works, sort of.

Though Cathy and Heathcliff still escape from the respective miseries of their domestic lives to dream away the days while they walk the moors, Cathy eventually falls in with a well-to-do family, the Lintons from Thrushcross

Grange. Cathy is flattered to find herself courted by young Edgar Linton, who eventually proposes marriage. Should she marry him? What about Heathcliff? When Heathcliff overhears Cathy discussing her dilemma with Nelly Dean—it would degrade her to marry Heathcliff, she says—he flees Wuthering Heights and doesn't return for three years. He should have stayed put and listened—right after the degradation bit Cathy goes on to say of Heathcliff: "He's more myself than I am. Whatever our souls are made of, his and mine are the same."

When Heathcliff does reintroduce himself to the story, his old flame Cathy (now surnamed Linton), finds him to be a handsome and wealthy young gentleman. Also impressed is Edgar Linton's sister, Isabella. Infatuated is a better word. Unfortunately for her, she succumbs and marries Heathcliff, who proposes in order to get revenge on Edgar Linton. Once married, he degrades Isabella and pauperizes Hindley, who becomes a drunkard. Heathcliff acquires Wuthering Heights through a gambling debt and makes Hindley's and Isabella's lives miserable. Meanwhile, on the other side of town, Cathy lies dying. In a scene made for the movies, Heathcliff has one more chance to embrace his love.

The next generation at Wuthering Heights fares somewhat better, as will you if you can keep track of them: Hareton Earnshaw is Hindley's son, Cathy Linton is Edgar and Catherine's daughter, and Linton Heathcliff is Heathcliff and Isabella's son. After Heathcliff has avenged himself on Edgar by swiping Edgar's daughter's inheritance (it cost him the life of his own son to do it), Cathy and Hareton fall in love and finally there's a happy ending.

THE YORKSHIRE MOORS

Haworth Village, York County, England.

The Yorkshire moors are part of a long English mountain range, the Pennines, which cut through parts of Yorkshire, including the village of Haworth where Patrick Brontë's parsonage was. The parsonage is now the site of the Brontë museum (T-shirts and postcards anyone?), but the moors are just as cold and desolate as ever. All three Brontë girls walked them endlessly, but only Emily seems to have had a spiritual connection with those miles of heather and gorse, as does her heroine, Catherine Linton.

A FORCE IS A FORCE, OF COURSE, OF COURSE

If you've seen the movie directed by William Wyler in 1939, it will be hard to reconcile your memory of the wonderfully youthful Lord Larry Olivier with the novel's portrait of Heathcliff-the-furious. In the movie, Heathcliff is wronged by Hindley and hence every indignity he causes others to suffer seems warranted. In the movie, you can understand why Catherine loves Heathcliff (everyone loved Olivier and some were foolish enough to act on it). The point of the *book*, however, is that Catherine's love for Heathcliff is inexplicable—even to Catherine herself.

When it came out in 1847, *Wuthering Heights* received profoundly negative reviews. Critics denounced the book as "a shocking picture of the worst form of brutality." Others found it "coarse and loathsome." Even sister Charlotte was hard-pressed to account for Heathcliff's character. No one had ever seen anything like it before.

THE PATHETIC FALLACY

John Ruskin (1819–1900).

This is a term the nineteenth-century British art critic John Ruskin used to note how writers and artists endow their depictions of nature with human qualities. Ruskin considered this a fault when done to excess, but one of the signal tendencies of Romantic writers was to see in nature an external projection of the landscape of their own souls. Emily Brontë reverses the idea: She starts instead with a piece of nature and imagines a human soul similar to it. Heathcliff's rocky temperament is meant to match the untamed storminess of the moors.

Maybe Satan in Milton's *Paradise Lost*, but at least you expected him to be so foul.

Emily also wrote some very fine poems, but *Wuthering Heights* was her one novel—the finest novel this estimable family produced. Here are the summaries of a few other novels of sister Anne, whose books are, among the three sisters', the least read, but have enduring value nonetheless.

ANNE'S *AGNES GREY*, AND *THE TENANT OF WILDFELL HALL*

The heroine of *Agnes Grey* tries futilely to tame her charges, the Bloomfields. Tom, the eldest, can't wait to ride a pony, and "cut into him like smoke" with his whip and spurs. To practice, he amuses himself by trapping birds (which he gives to cats, or cuts into pieces with his penknife while they are still alive). Encouraged by his father, Tom plans to roast a bird alive "to see how long it will live."

Her efforts to civilize the Bloomfield children a failure, Agnes Grey is dismissed. If only the Partridge Family had been hiring. Agnes feels only a little safer when she marries Edward Weston, a poor but devoted clergyman. She's certainly no wealthier.

The critics were put off by the gritty realities depicted in Anne's fiction, but she didn't give up. Anne's second novel, *The Tenant of Wildfell Hall*, came out in 1848. It's an epistolary novel told through a series of letters written by Gilbert Markham to his brother-in-law, and through the journal of the tenant, Helen Graham Huntingdon.

The Tenant of Wildfell Hall:
A LITERARY TOUT SHEET

Gilbert Markham: Narrates the story through a series of letters.

Helen Huntingdon: Wife of a womanizing drunkard. She does her duty as a wife but she is happy when Huntingdon finally kills himself from excessive drinking. In the end she marries Gilbert Markham.

Arthur Huntingdon: Makes his wife's life miserable with his hard drinking and fast friends. He even tries to corrupt his young son.

Her journal describes her bad marriage to Arthur Huntingdon, whose drunken debauches make Helen's life miserable. Huntingdon virtually imprisons her, fills the house with like-minded friends, takes a mistress, and tries to corrupt his young son. When his drinking finally kills Huntingdon, Helen is able to marry her longtime admirer, Gilbert Markham.

CHARLOTTE'S *VILLETTE*

In her final work, the autobiographical *Villette*, Charlotte Brontë again used Constantin Héger as a model for her

WHO'S HO ☞

Villette:
A LITERARY TOUT SHEET

Lucy Snowe: Heroine of the novel, a teacher in a Brussels boarding school, she is scared half to death by the ghostly appearance of a dead nun.

Madame Beck: Proprietress of Villette, the boarding school, hates Lucy, and succeeds in making the young teacher's life miserable. She is a thinly disguised version of the wife of Constantin Héger, the man Charlotte Brontë loved in vain.

Paul Emmanuel: A professor at Villette. Lucy falls in love with him and wins his affections despite the interference of Madame Beck. Unfortunately, at the end he is lost at sea and so are the readers. Brontë never tells us whether he resurfaces or not. Poor little Lucy just keeps waiting.

protagonist, Paul Emmanuel. Lucy Snowe, her heroine, teaches at Villette, a Brussels school, whose directoress is the scheming Madame Beck. Snowe finds love by winning over the sarcastic, embittered Professor Paul Emmanuel. In real life, alas, Charlotte did not win Héger. So obvious is Mme. Beck's resemblance to Héger's wife that Charlotte Brontë unsuccessfully tried to ban the book from foreign export—an unusual tactic for an author in want of money.

Madam Héger saw the book anyway, and never got over her bitterness about the scathing portrait of herself. She refused to give biographers information about the Brontës.

THE END OF THE LINE

Branwell's death in 1848 especially affected Emily, who was closest of the three sisters to their brother. Despite her own fragile health, she wore herself down nursing Branwell through his final illness, then caught a cold at his funeral and died three months later. A year after Emily's death, Anne died of consumption, leaving Charlotte to take care of their half-blind and weakening father.

Before *Villette* was published in 1854, Charlotte received a marriage proposal from her father's curate, Arthur Bell Nicholls. At last she felt happy, but her delicate health was broken by the pregnancy that followed. She died in March of 1855.

The Brontë sisters, Emily most forcefully, broke with the sentimental conventions of nineteenth-century fiction. Whereas in *Jane Eyre* Charlotte created a heroine who could have been the girl next door (if the girl next door had some of little Jane's gumption), Emily's Heathcliff was unlike anyone seen in fiction up to that time.

Emily Brontë's Suitcase.

SUMMARY

🕐 Three talented writers made careers out of a child-hood necessity to invent a world of their own.

🕐 Emily, the most talented, wrote only one novel, *Wuthering Heights.*

🕐 Charlotte used her early one-sided affair with Constantin Héger as the source and theme for most of her fiction.

🕐 Anne, the youngest, brought realism into her novels in her grim portrait of the life of a governess.

CHAPTER 3

MARY WOLLSTONECRAFT SHELLEY
(1797–1851)

YOU MUST REMEMBER THIS

Flaws and all, *Frankenstein* touched a nerve (as it were) at a time when both the Gothic novel and the notion of the spontaneous generation of life were hot.

MOST FAMOUS FOR

★ *Frankenstein* (1818)

66 **I** beheld the wretch—the miserable monster whom I had created."

The monster is: (1) Dr. Frankenstein's creation, a being eight feet tall with "watery eyes . . . shrivelled complexion . . . straight black lips" (and a bad haircut); or (2) the sometimes clumsy novel written by the twenty-year-old Mary Shelley, a book that had a seminal effect on the world of B-movies. The answer is both 1 and 2, depending on your taste. But keep in mind that anyone over the age of seven who enjoys tales of fantastical horror would be limited to reading *Consumer Reports*

Ol' Zipperneck—Boris Karloff brought Frankenstein's monster to the Hollywood screen and the twentieth-century collective unconscious.

were it not for Mary Wollstonecraft Godwin Shelley's *Frankenstein*.

THE CREATORS OF THE CREATRIX OF THE CREATURE

Mary Shelley was born to "glorious parents," as her husband Percy once rhapsodized. Her father was William Godwin, one of England's leading reformers and radical philosophers. Educated for the ministry, Mr. Godwin turned atheist and taught that society could not be reformed by religion, only by rational thinking. Rationally enough, he advocated the abolition of all institutions, including marriage. He did take a wife nonetheless: Mary Wollstonecraft, an early feminist who wrote *A Vindication of the Rights of Women*.

Mary Godwin, daughter of Mary Wollstonecraft, also succumbed to marriage. She chose a poet—Percy Bysshe Shelley. Mary's father, the radical advocate of free love, tried to break up the affair, so the couple chose to flee. They took along Claire Clairmont, Mary's stepsister, for ballast. The consequences of both decisions were dire. Godwin disowned his daughter, and Claire Clairmont became an insufferable burden.

The three then embarked on the European tour that began Mary's career as an author. She published an account of her trip under the elegantly simple title, *History of a Six Weeks Tour Through a Part of France, Switzerland, Germany and Holland*.

In the summer of 1822 the Shelleys, who had moved to Italy in 1818, took a house on Lake Spezia. Tragically,

Percy drowned in a sailing accident. The distraught Mary set about collecting her husband's poems, and began to write his biography. She canonized him, and pardoned his faults, writing that they "proved him to be human,

PERCY BYSSHE SHELLEY (1792–1822)

Percy Bysshe Shelley (1792–1822).
Angel-faced Romantic poet, Mary's husband.

Percy Shelley was already an important poet by the time he met Mary in 1814. Though best known today for his poetry (one eminent critic has called him "a lyrical poet without rival"), Shelley was also known in his own time for his radical political, religious, and sexual opinions. It's not surprising then that he was attracted to the Godwin family, especially since his own father had cut off his funds after the young poet was thrown out of Oxford ("sent down," the English say) for circulating a pamphlet entitled *The Necessity of Atheism*. A Platonist to the core, Shelley took Periclean Athens as his political standard. The same Plato who would have banished poets from The Republic might have found ironic Shelley's claim, in *The Defense of Poetry*, that poets are "the unacknowledged legislators of mankind."

without them, the exalted nature of his soul would have raised him into something divine.''

Worn out by repeated illnesses and exhaustion, Mary succumbed to a brain tumor on February 21, 1851. For the most part, she was mourned as Percy Shelley's widow. Only a few, like George Lewes, George Eliot's lover, recognized her as an important author in her own right. *Frankenstein* is good enough to have earned her that praise.

BEST-KNOWN NOVEL

When *Frankenstein* was published anonymously in 1818, it became quite a hit in literary London. Frankenstein, as you may recall, is not the monster, but the name of the scientist who made him. And as the full title, *Frankenstein, or the Modern Prometheus*, indicates, the story is about the scientist who didn't know enough to let sleeping limbs lie.

The novel opens with a series of letters from Robert Walton, an Arctic explorer, addressed to his sister in London, a Mrs. Saville. Walton relates how he has rescued Victor Frankenstein, a brilliant scientist who'd become lost in the polar region. Frankenstein dictated his story to Walton, and now Walton in turn includes that frightening tale in his letters.

In the course of Frankenstein's scientific researches and pseudoscientific practices (like alchemy), he learns the secret of creating life which, among other things, requires a good amount of toil with decomposing stiffs.

PROMETHEUS

Prometheus figures prominently in Greek mythology and literature, especially Aeschylus's *Prometheus Bound.* Prometheus was man's hero, chosen to steal the fire of creation so that man himself might become a creator. But since creation was a prerogative of the gods, Zeus punished Prometheus by fastening him to the side of a mountain where an eagle gnawed on his liver by day, but the indomitable organ grew back again every night. (You may wonder just who was being punished here—man or bird.)

Because the English Romantics prized the creative and imaginative faculties, the myth of Prometheus is central to their thinking. In fact, Percy Shelley wrote a verse play called *Prometheus Unbound,* the title of which more or less gives away the ending.

Guess who's coming to dinner? Prometheus awaits his torment.

He ransacks cadavers for usable parts in order to assemble his creation, and finally gives it life. The creator's pride turns to horror, which leads, in Frankenstein's case, to a brain fever that lasts two years.

In the meantime, the monster goes berserk and strangles the scientist's young brother. The authorities, however, believe the murderer is a young girl who had been one of the Frankenstein family's servants. Despite Victor's very best efforts to rescue the girl, she is hanged for the murder. Now there are two unfortunate deaths—and one unpardonable birth—for which Dr. Frankenstein is responsible.

Tormented thus by his own guilt, the doctor who can't wake the dead seeks solitude in order to salve his conscience. The plot must go on, however, and so the monster seeks out his creator and recounts his own tale of woe. First, the beast with twin bolts (in his neck, in the movie version) roamed the countryside seeking food and human companionship . . . with an unsurprising lack of success. We find out that he has learned to read, and has discovered thereby the horrible secret of his not-so-immaculate conception. The monster strikes a bargain with the credulous doctor. If Frankenstein will make the creature a mate, he will make himself scarce.

Frankenstein does produce the monster's dream date (out of odd scraps acquired after closing time at the morgue, we imagine). But in a fit of good judgment, Frankenstein destroys this blind date from hell. The lonely, mateless monster makes good a threat of retribution, strangling first one of the doctor's good friends, Clerval, and then Dr. Frankenstein's young bride. The

Frankenstein:
A LITERARY TOUT SHEET

Robert Walton: An English explorer and narrator of the story.

Victor Frankenstein: A brilliant scientist who creates a monster man.

The monster: The creation of Frankenstein, his loneliness drives him to pillage and murder.

Elizabeth: Frankenstein's bride, whom the monster murders on her wedding night.

scientist chases the monster northward, hoping to destroy it.

Cut to the North Pole, where Frankenstein is pursuing the brute he spawned. Here Walton finds Dr. Frankenstein, hell-bent for revenge. Shortly after Frankenstein finishes his sorry tale, he dies. Then, the beast himself boards Walton's ship and talks about plans for a big funeral fire where he will immolate himself along with the corpse of his creator. But the creature changes his mind, leaps onto an ice floe, and is never heard from again. Well, almost never: in less than a hundred years, the advent of cinema would elevate the sad creature into the cultural pantheon of the undead.

THE WRITER IN HER LABORATORY

It is unlikely that you will ever receive a 250-page letter. But if you do, it is even more improbable that this hypothetical missive will be broken down into book chapters as is the lengthy letter from Walton to his sister. And yet, Mary Shelley manages to make the letter form work as a novelistic device to create an intimacy between a writer and a reader that is otherwise difficult to achieve.

George Gordon, Lord Byron (1788–1824), Don Juan of the nineteenth-century literary set.

An epic poet may seek to inspire his audience through an expansive, grand style, one suited perhaps to declaiming sweeping verses in a crowded amphitheater of yore. For a ghost story to work, however, an author must establish a more intimate atmosphere aimed at an audience of one or more listeners in the mood for a scare. It was in a spooky environment such as this that *Frankenstein* was invented. As it occurred a few friends had gathered one night around a fireplace in the Italian villa of Lord Byron, a decadent nobleman who also happened to be one of the most famous poets of that or any other age. As the wine flowed, the master of the house challenged each guest to invent a tale of supernatural horror. Mary recalled a dream she'd had about a huge monster, and began to set pen to paper.

Frankenstein thrilled Mary Shelley's immediate audience—those vacationers in the villa. And when the book was finally published a few years later, the reading public took to it with equal enthusiasm. *Frankenstein* was, indeed, the first science fiction novel as well as the forerunner of all the bestselling horror stories to come, notably Robert Louis Stevenson's *The Strange Case of Dr. Jekyll and Mr. Hyde.* Shelley's tale, however, is more than a sensational novel. What she was trying to prove was that human nature is essentially good until it's corrupted by ill-treatment. Frankenstein's monster becomes violent only when he is repelled by "civilized" human beings who shudder at his grotesque features. His loneliness drives him to acts of unspeakable horror. The tale evoked sympathy for the "noble savage" so celebrated

THE EPISTOLARY NOVEL

If you've read *The Color Purple* you'll recall that Alice Walker used letters between her characters to advance the story. In adopting this format, she drew on a distinguished literary tradition. The eighteenth century was the heyday of the epistolary novel. *Clarissa*, Samuel Richardson's impossibly long novel (coming in at over one million words, it's the longest in the English language), concerns a young woman of virtue and her seducer, both of whom are responsible for most of the correspondence. And in France, Jean-Jacques Rousseau credited *Clarissa* as the inspiration for his own epistolary novel, *Julie, ou la Nouvelle Héloise.*

Most epistolary novels depend on an exchange of letters. *Frankenstein* distinguishes itself in this regard as the work of a unilateral correspondent: we never do learn what Walton's sister felt about receiving such a load of morbid news.

THE GOTHIC NOVEL

Frankenstein belongs to the tradition of the Gothic novel. Horace Walpole is given credit as the genre's originator with his novel *The Castle of Otranto.* The genre is called Gothic because so many of the novels that fall under this heading are set against a background of medieval castles and other examples of Gothic architecture. Though *Frankenstein* uses no such props, the other trappings of the genre are here: violence, horror, supernatural effects, and a pallid, denatured sexuality.

Nathaniel Hawthorne and Edgar Allan Poe are two American practitioners of Gothic fiction, and in our own day Joyce Carol Oates has had some success with similar themes. Finally, in the world of mass-market paperbacks there exists an entire subgenre called Gothic Romance. A little-known publishing industry convention dictates that such "Gothics" signal their genre to readers through covers that show a nervous heroine at night in front of a big dark house that has one light shining in an upper-story window.

by the romantic poets, particularly Wordsworth and Coleridge.

FUTURE FRANKENSTEIN

Despite a plethora of imitations, *Frankenstein* endures. The style is often florid and sometimes graceless. But you can argue that Mary Shelley's breathless style befits the extravagant supernatural theme she chose. Moreover, in the early nineteenth century, readers responded favorably to the wind of earnest, intense expression that today's critics would call overwritten. Despite the twists Shelley gives her plot, the story is one of the oldest in the realm of human affairs, namely, the fact that one's creations often take on a life of their own. Go back to the book of Genesis, where God creates Adam and Eve and soon has reason to be displeased with His handiwork. There's also the legend of Pygmalion, or *My Fair Lady*, where Dr. Henry Higgins remakes Eliza Doolittle in his own sophisticated image. Or recall the well-intentioned girl in high school who saw the "good heart" underneath a felon-in-training's tough exterior, and turned the juvenile delinquent into a married man with a mortgage.

Mary Shelley's one great novel spawned a phrase, "to create a Frankenstein," which we apply today to everything from celebrity rock stars run amok, to government agencies that harass the public they're meant to serve. On a more serious note, the novel offers lessons that resonate in our era, most notably in the matter of human injustice. Society sometimes makes "Frankensteins" of the disadvantaged, whether they're people who are disfigured, or who just don't fit in. Mary Shelley dramatizes the anguish caused by such prejudice in a way that has rarely been surpassed.

OTHER WORKS

Although Mary Shelley wrote six other novels, *Frankenstein* was a hard act to follow. One of her subsequent works, *Mathilda*, is the story of an incestuous relationship

between a father and a daughter. Strangely, the plot also
concerns the love affair of the heroine and a poet who
abandoned her. Percy Shelley never left Mary, but otherwise a psychological interpretation of the book would
suggest that Mathilda is a projection of the author's
grievances, as the plot of *Mathilda* bears a notable simi-
larity to her own life.

Four years passed before Mary Shelley wrote another
novel. In 1826 she published *The Last Man*, another
proto-science fiction tale which, among her works, ranks
second to *Frankenstein* in popularity. Adrian, a Percy

BREAKFAST WITH THE SHELLEYS

Shelley-like hero, is the son of a British king. The monarch abdicates his throne. Although Adrian would rather study and write poetry (a notion less trite then than it is now), he gives in to his countrymen's plea to accept the position of Lord Protector of England because a plague has devastated Europe. Despite his efforts, only three people, including himself, survive on earth after the terrible epidemic, and ultimately just one, the narrator Lionel Verney, survives to tell the tale.

SUMMARY

 The daughter of famous parents, the wife of a famous husband, Mary Shelley is herself a key figure in the history of English Romanticism.

 Frankenstein was an up-to-date rendering of the myth of Prometheus, the fire-stealer, hence the subtitle: ". . . or the modern Prometheus."

 Frankenstein, a forerunner of the modern horror and science-fiction novel, is as significant for its influence on popular culture as it is for its achievement as literature.

 Had she not written *Frankenstein*, Mary Shelley would be remembered chiefly as the wife of Percy Bysshe Shelley.

CHAPTER 4

CHARLES DICKENS
(1812–1870)

YOU MUST REMEMBER THIS

He vividly depicted the working class of British society in the Victorian era. Achieved immense popularity in his lifetime by providing a rich array of memorable, often humorous characters, while showing the dark side of the Industrial Revolution as it affected the average man.

MOST FAMOUS FOR

Producing more novels (14) than children (10). Here is a list of the novels:

★ *Oliver Twist*: 1838
★ *Nicholas Nickleby*: 1839
★ *The Old Curiosity Shop*: 1840
★ *Barnaby Rudge*: 1841
★ *A Christmas Carol*: 1843
★ *Martin Chuzzlewit*: 1844
★ *Dombey and Son*: 1848

★ *David Copperfield*: 1850
★ *Bleak House*: 1853
★ *Hard Times*: 1854
★ *Little Dorrit*: 1857
★ *A Tale of Two Cities*: 1859
★ *Great Expectations*: 1861
★ *Our Mutual Friend*: 1865

Dickens died before completing a fifteenth novel,
The Mystery of Edwin Drood.

Y ou know eccentrics. Your next-door neighbor mows the lawn in the buff. Your brother-in-law claims he's on a first-name basis with the Pope. Are these characters Dickensian, or just certifiably nuts?

IT WAS THE BEST OF LIVES, IT WAS THE WORST OF LIVES

The second of eight children, Dickens was forced by his mother to work in a shoe polish factory, even after the family finances began to improve. She must have thought this labor built character in the same way that violin lessons did for Dickens's sister Fanny. Dickens was more kindly disposed toward his father, even though the old man did time in a debtors' prison. For one thing, his father got him out of the shoe polish industry and insisted that Dickens continue his education instead. Young Charles won a prize in Latin and read widely. Among his favorites were Shakespeare and Tobias Smollet.

Dickens finished with his schooling at fifteen, and went to work as a clerk in a law office. His uncle taught him shorthand and got him a job as a news reporter on the staff of the *Morning Chronicle*. Here he absorbed the sights and sounds of London, which he incorporated in his first serious novel, *Oliver Twist*, published in 1838.

Dickens had less luck in marriage than he did in literature. In 1836, the same year he republished articles from periodicals *Sketches by Boz*, the young author met his future wife, Catherine Hogarth, the eldest daughter of his editor. Though their marriage a year later eventually

TOBIAS SMOLLETT (1721–1771)

Tobias Smollett (1721–1771).

One of Dickens's literary influences, this writer at first tried and failed to make a living as a playwright. The Scottish-born novelist also served as a surgeon's mate aboard a ship. Tobias Smollett's first novel, *The Adventures of Roderick Random*, is based on his seafaring adventures. Other novels include *Peregrine Pickle, Ferdinand Count Fathom,* and *Humphrey Clinker.* Best known for his portrayal of eccentric characters, Smollet explained what he thought a novel must be: ". . . a large diffused picture, comprehending the characters of life. . . . But this plan cannot be executed . . . without a principal personage to attract the attention . . . unwind the clue of the labyrinth, and at last close the scene, by virtue of his own importance." Dickens seems to have taken this advice to heart, for his unforgettable eye-catching characters are the magnets that draw readers through his sprawling dramas.

produced ten children, Dickens soon realized that he and his beloved had nothing in common, aside from a passel of little ones. Dickens was irritated by his wife's complacency, obesity, and slovenliness. She, in turn, suffered the humiliation of her husband's numerous love affairs, particularly with an actress, Ellen Ternan.

Dickens was famous for becoming emotionally involved with his fictional characters. When working on

ELLEN TERNAN (1839–1907)

The youngest daughter of theatrical parents, Ellen Ternan met Dickens when she was eighteen years old. The affair lasted until Dickens's death in 1870. Dickens kept the liaison a secret from all but his intimate friends and his wife, who learned that Dickens was sending Ellen expensive jewelry. He bought a house for the Ternan family and visited Ellen under an assumed name.

a novel, Dickens would become so wrapped up in his characters' lives that he'd speak their dialogue out loud, acting each part and so engaging in boisterous confrontations with himself. He admitted weeping over the death of Little Nell in *The Old Curiosity Shop*. Such vivacity charged his real life as well: Dickens loved parties, playing with children, and acting in home theatricals— mayhap Ellen Ternan helped him rehearse the love scenes. He liked to travel, dance, and entertain.

In the 1850s Dickens founded his own magazine, *Household Words*, a weekly publication that, like Dickens, provided entertainment with a social conscience. In 1858 he began to give public readings, and he journeyed to America for this purpose. The lectures were profitable, but physically draining. His last novel, *Edwin Drood* (the subject of a recent Broadway play) was never finished. He died on June 9, 1870, and was buried in the Poets' Corner at London's Westminster Abbey.

**WHO'S
WHO** ☛

The Novels
of Charles Dickens:

A LITERARY TOUT SHEET TO THE FAVORITES AND THE LONG SHOTS

Dickens's characters are seldom gray. The heroes are goody-goodies and the villains perfectly odious, yet both are memorable. Here is a list of the most famous heroes and heroines from his novels:

Oliver: The poor orphan who never lost his virtue or his optimism, in *Oliver Twist*.

Sidney Carton: He gave up his life for the woman he loved in *A Tale of Two Cities*.

Nicholas Nickleby: A teacher who tried to reform the corrupt school system. From the novel of the same name.

Little Nell of *The Old Curiosity Shop* is literally too good for this world. She took care of her aged grandfather and beat off the advances of an evil dwarf. When she dies at the end, the public, as well as Dickens, went into mourning.

Ebenezer Scrooge: When a miser reforms, he has to become a hero. Who can forget *A Christmas Carol*, the most famous of Christmas stories?

WHO'S WHO ☞

(*continued*)

"OK. You're the Ghost of Christmas Present. Quite amusing. Now go away!"

Florence Dombey of *Dombey and Son* took a lot of abuse from her father just because she wasn't a boy.

David Copperfield: A hero who most resembled Dickens himself. The novel, named after the hero, contains a most memorable eccentric character, Micawber, who never had a job because he was always "waiting for something to turn up."

Amy Dorrit: Called "Little Dorrit" (the title of the novel) because of her size. She was born in debtors' prison and spent most of her life trying to pay off her father's debts.

WHO'S WHO ☞

(*continued*)

And now a list of infamous villains (You'll like them better!):

Fagin: He teaches Oliver Twist and other kids how to steal.

Bill Sykes: In *Oliver Twist* he murders his girlfriend, Nancy.

Daniel Quilp: A repulsive dwarf in *The Old Curiosity Shop.* He impoverishes an old man and then tries to seduce his granddaughter, Little Nell.

Uriah Heep: In *David Copperfield,* he is the symbol of a hypocrite, who steals his employer's business.

Madame Defarge: The bloodthirsty French revolutionist who seeks the lives of all aristocrats, even the innocent ones, in *A Tale of Two Cities.*

Mrs. Joe: A shrew in *Great Expectations.* Other villains, include Bentley Drummle, and a character named Compeyson who deserted Miss Havisham on her wedding day and later tries to cheat Pip out of his inheritance.

Wackford Squeers: A money-hungry sadist, the head of a private school in *Nicholas Nickleby.*

Tulkinghorn: A blackmailing lawyer who seeks to become rich by threatening to reveal the secret love life of a grande dame in *Bleak House.*

BEST-KNOWN NOVEL

Great Expectations

Young Philip Pirrip, known as Pip, is an orphan who's been raised by his sister and her loyal husband, Joe Gargery, the local blacksmith. One evening at Christmastime, while out visiting the graves of his parents, Pip is surprised by an escaped convict who coerces him to steal food from Mrs. Joe. Though the convict is soon recaught by the authorities, he is destined to play an ongoing role in young Pip's life.

Miss Havisham is a wealthy and eccentric old bird who pays for Pip to come and play with Estella, her ward. Estella displays a contempt for the rough working-class lad, which seems to have been Miss Havisham's intent for she invites Pip to come play again. Although he's insulted at every turn, Pip is intrigued with the upper-class style. Eventually Havisham pays for Pip's indenture papers so that Pip may be officially apprenticed to Joe. Yet Pip's brief visits with Miss Havisham and Estella have convinced him that he wants something besides the life of a common rustic.

His dream is fulfilled when a formidable lawyer named Mr. Jaggers informs Pip that he's "a young gentleman of great expectations" who is going to inherit a great sum of money. There are a few conditions: he has to leave Joe and Mrs. Joe, he must always bear the name Pip, and can never ask the identity of his benefactor. Deal?

Pip comes to London and quickly befriends Herbert Pocket, the son of his tutor. Other young men in the

---

INDENTURED SERVITUDE . . . .

Indentured servitude was a common practice in the
eighteenth and nineteenth centuries. Anyone desiring
to learn a trade had to first serve an apprenticeship
with a master or skilled worker who owned his shop. In
order to become an apprentice one had to sign a contract with the employer or master. In exchange for instruction, the apprentice worked long hours for no pay.
Usually, the apprenticeship lasted seven years, after
which time the apprentice became a journeyman. Then
he traveled from place to place selling the goods he
made. For this he received some salary. The only way
an apprentice could break his contract was by paying
off his employer.

---

boarding establishment Pip now calls home are Startop
and a boor by the name of Bentley Drummle.

Pip is convinced that it is Miss Havisham who has set
him up as a young gentleman-in-training. She's the only
person he knows who has enough money to pull it off,
and surely she wants Pip to marry Estella. Actually, Miss
Havisham is busy hardening Estella's heart against all
men: this beautiful young girl is Miss Havisham's revenge
on the male sex. We learn that Havisham was jilted on
her wedding day and has worn her yellowing bridal gown
ever after to keep alive the flame of anger that the hu-
miliating event implanted in her breast.

Pip's benefactor turns out to be Magwitch, the convict
from the cemetery who has come now to London to see
the gentleman he helped create. Magwitch made quite
a fortune as a sheep farmer in Australia, where he'd

been sent as a convict. (Remember your history—
Australia was once an English penal colony.) What kept
the old con working so hard was the memory of the boy
who took pity on him "an' 'elped 'im out." Pip is initially appalled to learn that his benefactor has been a
convicted criminal. To make matters worse, it is realized
that Magwitch ought not to have returned, for now his
appearance in London has roused the suspicions of the
authorities. Pip and Herbert plot to get Magwitch on
board a ship, and Pip plans to join him.

Here's where Dickens really gets busy: Pip goes to visit
Miss Havisham one last time. By way of an apology for
her cruelty to Pip (and Estella), she promises to help
provide the capital to establish Herbert Pocket, Pip's
good friend, in a career. At this juncture her wedding
dress catches fire, a pyrotechnic event that leaves Havisham on her deathbed. Pip then discovers the secret of
Estella's parentage: Magwitch is her father, and Molly,
the rough and ready housekeeper of that lawyer, Mr.
Jaggers, is her mother. Jaggers suggests that this is a secret better kept between themselves. It comes time for
Pip and Magwitch to board their escape boat, but the
pair are waylaid by the malevolent Compeyson, the man
responsible for Magwitch's imprisonment, and (believe
it or not) the same bloke who jilted Miss Havisham!

Magwitch is tried, found guilty, and is set to be
hanged. But before the sentence can be carried out, he
gets in a fight with Compeyson. Though mortally
wounded, Magwitch lingers long enough for Pip to tell
Magwitch that his daughter Estella lives and Pip loves
her. Pip has run up some serious debt and with all of
Magwitch's money confiscated has no way to pay it back.

As luck would have it, Pip falls ill so his creditors will have to wait to put him in jail. Joe has come to London to nurse Pip back to health and pay off his debts with the little money he's saved as a smith. Pip recovers and goes East for some time with Herbert and his missus. On his return to England more than a decade later, he visits what was once Miss Havisham's house (she, of course, is dead and the house has been torn down) and sees Estella. She had been married to Drummle, now dead. Pip and she are reunited, and as Pip says, he sees "no shadow of another parting from her."

IT'S A SMALL WORLD AFTER ALL

Yes, it's a small world, but to account for all the coincidences and neat turns in this book the earth would have to be about the size of a matchbook. The London Dickens knew was surely bigger than that. So why the dizzying array of coincidences?

The answer has to do with how the author wrote his novels. Dickens's works were originally published in serial form—that is, in magazines. A certain number of words were demanded of him each month. To fulfill his responsibilities, he made plots up on the fly and had little time to rewrite. Once he put a character into the action, that personage was there for the rest of the book. Dickens's novels ramble enough as it is; to make them cohere he used his characters like dots in a very large circle and then connected those dots as he approached the end. In this sense, despite some twists that may be hard to believe, the novels are indeed masterful artistic achievements. And one great advantage, as Dickens saw it, was that this braiding of disparate threads and then the closure, or tidying up, satisfied his readers immensely.

You cannot underestimate the importance readers played in Dickens's literary career. Today, all you hear are authors complaining that no one reads their books. Dickens knew his were read. Readers responded immediately to each section of each novel as it was published in magazine form. Often, as word got back to him about his readers' reception of the latest installment, Dickens did actually shape the plot so as not to disappoint them.

The greatest drawback to serial publication was that, since it afforded him very little time to reconsider his work, he could not produce books that were as polished as Jane Austen's, for example. Whereas her novels are dense with psychological insight and carefully directed motives, Dickens's are not. His characters are distinctive but lack depth. When Dickens's characters speak, you'll rarely detect multiple layers of meaning in their words (for example, sarcasm or irony). There's no tragic flaw, no sexual turmoil waiting to surface; in short, these figures are short on psychological complexity.

To make up for what his novels lacked in such depth, Dickens often enriches his characterizations by having one player recall an incident that illuminates the personality of another. For instance, when *Bleak House*'s protagonist, Esther Summerson, remembers an evening spent at the home of the slovenly Mrs. Jellyby, Dickens can evoke another impression of this woman who neglects her children in order to study social conditions in Africa.

Dickens was essentially a caricaturist. He learned early

WHO'S WHO ☞

Great Expectations:
A LITERARY TOUT SHEET

Joe Gargery: Simple, good-hearted blacksmith, is kind to his wife's young brother, Pip.

Mrs. Joe: A real harridan, treats her husband with contempt and her orphaned brother with cruelty.

Philip Pirrip: Otherwise known as Pip, he is the main character of the story. As he grows up, he has great expectations of becoming a "gentleman." He falls in love with a girl who treats him like dirt.

Abel Magwitch: A convict who befriends Pip.

Miss Havisham: A "Charles Addams" character who tries to make all men pay because she was disillusioned by one.

Estella: A haughty beauty trained by Miss Havisham to break men's hearts. Pip was one of her victims.

Herbert Pocket: Pip's faithful friend.

Bentley Drummle: A real cad who marries Estella and humbles her. She loses her hauteur but finds love with Pip.

on to give characters a verbal tick or mannerism that readers could easily recall—perhaps a particular dialect he'd heard walking the various districts of London, or maybe a phrase a character used again and again (in *Hard Times,* Gradgrind is always talking of "facts"—just like Joe Friday of the television series "Dragnet." In *Great Expectations,* a minor character named Wemmick refers to his father as "the Aged P."). This technique was a sort of shorthand that helped Dickens place a certain character in a social milieu, or indicate something about that character's personality.

In addition to such stylistic tricks, the writer had another, more natural gift. He was a master of dialect, a surprisingly difficult technique to master—maybe only our own Mark Twain rivals him. So, in *Great Expectations,* why does Pip have no accent? By the time he narrated the story, Pip is a grown man who has thrown off his country manners and his lower-class accent. In this novel, Dickens is interested in showing not how Pip speaks, but how his inner self evolves.

It takes Pip quite some time to recognize that Joe, the humble blacksmith, is one of the best men he's ever likely to meet. Pip frequently makes the mistake of assuming that a person's outer shell accurately represents his inner being. The boy learns that Herbert wasn't inept, he himself was; and Estella, though beautiful, is not so worthy of his affection until her soul has been softened by the hard ways of the world.

Again and again Dickens drives this point home: You cannot judge people by the way they appear. Compeyson is the rat dressed like a gent, and Magwitch is the magnanimous soul who looks like a felon no matter how well

CARICATURISTS

Caricature by Daumier.

Don't be misled, caricature is a serious art. In the nineteenth century, especially in France and England, caricaturists were highly respected, popular artists whose satires of contemporary society often served as instruments of social change. The French artist Honoré Daumier both drew and sculpted prominent Parisian figures, including small iron casts of the somber members of the French Chamber of Deputies. Daumier's caricatures, by seizing upon and then exaggerating certain outstanding or representative physical qualities, make the Deputies seem less than the imposing figures they thought they were.

Dickens, too, created characters whose salient features were blown out of human proportion. That is why a person who behaves in a noticeably outlandish way can often be described as "Dickensian."

At certain historical moments, exaggeration is the only way to make a point; and some of Dickens's creations were so powerful that they did. For instance, the portrayal of the malicious Fagin in *Oliver Twist* helped change child labor laws in England. Gary Trudeau, creator of the comic strip "Doonesbury," is an example of a caricaturist at work in our own age.

he's decked out. Pip learns this lesson the hard way. Through suffering and hardship, he not only sees people as they really are, but he realizes his false values and his stubbornness. When Pip gradually abandons the security and worldly success that Magwitch's money has guaranteed him, he learns to respect the inner value of others.

A FEW OTHER NOVELS BRIEFLY DISCUSSED

Oliver Twist

Oliver, an orphan, is mistreated and underfed by the workhouse officials, especially the cruel Bumble. He runs away to London where he falls in with a group of young thieves headed by the villain Fagin, who teaches the boys how to steal. After much intrigue and even a murder, Oliver's parentage is established and he is rescued by a benevolent old gentleman, Mr. Brownlow. The novel made such an impression on the Italian composer, Puccini, that he contemplated writing an opera about it. At the last minute he changed his mind and wrote *Turandot* instead.

David Copperfield

David Copperfield (1850) is partly autobiographical. David, sent by his cruel stepfather to London, makes a living labeling bottles. He lives with the kindly though impoverished Mr. Micawber (played by W. C. Fields in the classic movie made of this book) and Micawber's family. David eventually has some literary success, but neither that nor his scatterbrained wife, Dora (inspiration for the expression "Dumb Dora") bring him much pleasure. Dora, however, conveniently dies, leaving him free to fall in love with Agnes, a young woman whose father is in debt to the virulent Uriah Heep. With Micawber's help, David

Mr. Micawber and family in a scene from David Copperfield.

gives the evil Heep just punishment and marries Agnes. Like other Dickens's novels, this book exposed the inhuman cruelties of an industrialized nineteenth-century England.

Bleak House

The opening few paragraphs of *Bleak House* contain some of Dickens's finest prose. The book is centered around the interminable legal case *Jarndyce v. Jarndyce*, whose original point of contention is practically forgotten (Dickens's experience as a legal reporter stood him in good stead here). The case is finally settled in favor of

"It's a proposal for a new show on renovating old Victorian homes. We get a host that looks like Charles Dickens and we call it This Old Bleak House.*"*

a character named Richard Carstone, but all the money was used to litigate the case. Although Carstone dies, his wife Ada lives on at Bleak House with their son.

The Old Curiosity Shop

The Old Curiosity Shop (1840) was Dickens's most sentimental novel. Little Nell Trent lives with her grandfather in a small antique shop that he keeps to eke out a spare existence for them both. They are persecuted by the hideous dwarf, Daniel Quilp, from whom the grandfather borrowed money. Quilp seizes the shop and hounds Nell and her grandfather until both die of malnutrition and exhaustion. Quilp is Dickens's most grotesque villain, and Little Nell his most beloved heroine. The death of Little Nell brought such an outcry from the public that the author was tempted to bring her back to life.

DICKENS ON STAGE

The Frozen Deep (1857) was a three act play which Dickens wrote in collaboration with Wilkie Collins. The play takes place during a polar expedition on which our hero Richard Wardour, rejected suitor of the lovely Clara Burnham, rescues one Frank Aldersley, who happens to be the man Clara loves. (Got all that?) Wardour dies from hunger and exposure after bringing his rival to the arms of Clara. On stage Dickens played the part of Wardour; Collins played the successful suitor Aldersley. *The Frozen Deep* was a box-office failure, but its story of thwarted romance, noble sacrifice, a hero and his double, provided Dickens with the inspiration for the plot of his successful novel *A Tale of Two Cities* (1859), wherein English lawyer Sydney Carton goes to the guillotine in place of his look-alike Charles Darnay (a.k.a. the Marquis St. Evremonde), so that Darnay can live happily ever after with Lucie Manette, whom Carton loves. The play also marked the beginning of Dickens's liaison with the actress Ellen Ternan, who had a minor part in the drama.

DICKENS *V.* DICKENS

Dickens's novels were probably responsible for felling more trees than all the legal briefs composed by all the several generations of barristers involved in *Bleak Houses*'s Jarndyce v. Jarndyce. How can an author so popular— and so prolific—be so good? In fact, the Dickens cult did much to hurt his critical reputation in his own day. Many of his readers were from the same social classes he wrote about—the poor, the downtrodden, the meek, and the overwhelmed. Critics generally can't abide an author with such a readership, especially with a Thackeray around writing novels that seemed much more elegant than Dickens's improvisations. But currents in criticism change, and writers in the early part of our own century became more interested in books with a political purpose. There was decidedly a need for a novel of reform. Dickens, at first hand, knew the horrors of child labor from his days of servitude in a shoe polish factory. He was acutely aware of the degradation of debtors' prison, where his own father was a frequent inmate. He found a receptive audience as he spun off novel after novel decrying myriad injustices, including poverty, corruption, inferior education, mistreatment of orphans, unconscionable delays in the legal system, and the exploitation of the lower class. At last the public woke up and demanded social reform. Dickens's reputation rose again. The general reader's love for Dickens has never flagged. The true test of any book is whether or not it stays fixed in a reader's memory and Dickens's do. Most of his characters may be one-dimensional as they appear in his novels, but they live on as real people in our lives—Oliver Twist, Scrooge, Little Nell, Micawber, and a rich assortment of others.

SUMMARY

 Worked hard (fourteen novels is damn hard) to overcome his humble beginnings.

 Wrote for serial publication.

 Created eccentric characters that you'll never forget.

 Wrote to reform horrendous social abuses, such as child labor and debtors' prison.

CHAPTER 5

WILLIAM MAKEPEACE THACKERAY

(1811–1863)

YOU MUST REMEMBER THIS

In this author's time, his popularity rivalled Dickens's. Had he produced as many novels as Dickens, it still might today.

MOST FAMOUS FOR

- ★ *Vanity Fair* (1847)
- ★ *Pendennis* (1848)
- ★ *The Newcomes* (1855)
- ★ *Henry Esmond* (1852)
- ★ *The Virginians* (1859)

OH CALCUTTA!

Thackeray was born in Calcutta, India, in 1811, to upper-middle-class parents. He was scarcely four years old when his father died. A year later his mother sent him to a typical boarding school where, in the author's words, "a petty tyrant governed"—just like colonial India. In letters to his mother, the son complained of being treated "everyday with such manifest unkindness and injustice that I really can scarcely bear it. . . . There are but 370 boys in the school, I wish there were only 369."

When he entered Trinity College, Cambridge, Thackeray studied little but read a good deal, and wrote comic pieces for the undergraduate magazine. He left Cambridge after a year to travel, gamble, and dawdle about in idle company, all of which would eventually earn him nothing but an unofficial degree in Debauchery and Indolence (unfortunately, that major is seldom found anymore, but one can pursue it independently).

Thackeray studied law briefly, and then decided he wanted to paint, so he moved to Paris to study art. There he met and fell in love with Isabella Shaw, the seventeen-year-old daughter of an Irish army officer's impoverished widow. His mother-in-law was such a formidable pain in the arse that throughout his career Thackeray used her for his caricatures of domineering mothers-in-law. In one of his public readings of *The Newcomes*, when he reached a description of the tyrannical Mrs. Mackenzie, Thackeray broke off to say, "That's my she devil of a mother-in-law, you know."

Gambling debts and poor investments made Thack-

A scene from The Newcomes.

eray consider a serious career. But he didn't consider it seriously enough, for the man became a writer instead. Like Chekhov and Woody Allen, he began as a comic. He wrote sketches for *Bentley's* and other magazines, where he honed the talent for caricature that would make him famous.

In 1836 he had enough income, but not enough sense, to avoid marriage to Isabella. This union, like the one that afflicted Dickens, was a disaster. Isabella spent most of her married life in a mental hospital, and her husband was temporarily obliged to send their two children to live with his mother.

It was not until 1847, when he was thirty-six years old, that Thackeray published his first novel—*Vanity Fair*, a picaresque novel that made him formidably famous, rated second only to Charles Dickens in the pantheon of living English novelists.

PICARESQUE NOVEL
Pronounced pick-are-ESK, not picturesque, it comes from the Spanish word *picaro*, which means "rogue." Not surprisingly, it's a Spanish genre (there are more rogues in Spain than there is coal in Newcastle) in which the hero of the novel is a rogue or vagabond. Other examples? Henry Fielding's *Tom Jones*, Mark Twain's *Huckleberry Finn*, and the mobster Henry Hill in the movie *Goodfellas*.

BEST-KNOWN NOVEL

Vanity Fair

Becky Sharp is crafty, unpleasant, and intelligent. She needs to be—she's the daughter of a poor drawing teacher. Only her wealthy friend Amelia Sedley can afford to be dull and merely well-intentioned. Becky schemes to marry Amelia's wealthy, indolent brother,

VANITY FAIR

The name comes from John Bunyan's religious allegory *The Pilgrim's Progress*, published in 1678. As Thackeray's novel is set in London, the title refers not to a particular place, but to an idea. Who aspires to material gain and social status is said to hold the ideals of Vanity Fair. The phrase connotates the frivolous values of those who weigh their decisions in matters of fashion as if they were matters of life and death. Such people moved with self-conscious ease through the elaborately mannered high society of Victorian England.

The title came to Thackeray, so he claimed, in his sleep one night. He jumped out of bed and ran around his room three times uttering "Vanity Fair, Vanity Fair, Vanity Fair."

John Bunyan (1628–1688),
author of The Pilgrim's Progress.

Joseph Sedley, a most graceless oaf. Amelia's sweetheart, George Osborne, thwarts Becky's plan—not out of loyalty to the Sedley clan, but because his high opinion of himself couldn't bear the burden of a formerly impoverished ex-governess for a sister-in-law.

Becky instead marries Rawdon Crawley who, because of his poor choice in a wife, is quickly disinherited by his wealthy aunt. Likewise, George Osborne's father dis-

THE BATTLE OF WATERLOO

June 18, 1815: In a small town, Waterloo, south of Brussels, the Allied forces decisively defeated the 72,000 French troops led by Napoleon Bonaparte. The combined German, Dutch, and British forces numbered roughly 67,000 under the command of Arthur Wellesley, duke of Wellington; the Prussians, famous for their military prowess, threw in another 50,000. Waterloo marked the beginning of the end for Napoleon; his escape from exile (the famous phrase, ABLE WAS I ERE I SAW ELBA, describes his fate; it is a palindrome: that is, it has the same meaning when read backward) was all undone when his seizure of power ended a little more than a week later with the restoration of Louis XVIII.

Thackeray's treatment of this historical event is typical of his method. Rather than ponder the wide-ranging political consequences of the battle, he takes you to the trenches and renders the small acts of bravery and cowardice that really make up a war. The impression Waterloo makes on his various characters is direct and personal.

inherits his son for marrying Amelia Sedley. Why? The Sedleys had money when this novel began, but they're paupered less than a third of the way through it—making Amelia an unsuitably moneyless match.

The romantic careers of the two male leads are interrupted at this stage by the Battle of Waterloo (June, 1815). Afterward, Joseph Sedley claims to have distinguished himself at Waterloo. He did not; in fact, he ran

*Napoleon's defeat at Waterloo—a scene
Kenneth Branagh would kill to direct.*

as fast as his fat little legs could carry him. George Osborne, who dies in action, can only claim a plot of land for his corpse. With George dead, Amelia and her son would have starved were it not for the generosity of Wil-

WHO'S WHO

Vanity Fair:
A LITERARY TOUT SHEET

Rebecca Sharp: A poor girl who lives by her wits by cultivating rich friends and scheming to marry their relatives.

Amelia Sedley: A Dickens-type heroine, good, pretty, sweet but dumb. She is used by Becky.

Jos Sedley: Amelia's fat, lazy, and stupid brother. He falls under Becky's spell and later is probably killed by her for his insurance money.

Rawdon Crawley: A "ne'er-do-well," Becky's husband. He conveniently dies of yellow fever.

George Osborne: Amelia's caddish husband, whom she adores until she finds out what a louse he is. He also conveniently dies—as a hero at the Battle of Waterloo, leaving Amelia free to marry.

William Dobbin: Who loves Amelia from afar, befriends her, and marries her at the end.

liam Dobbin, a devoted friend of George's since school, even though George was embarrassed by Dobbin's low social status.

When Rawdon Crawley discovers that his wife, the former Miss Becky Sharp, is taking money from gentleman callers, an unpleasant confrontation ensues. He then heads off to Coventry Island, where he will subsequently die of yellow fever. His little boy, Rawdy, is left to the mother who never cared for him at all. In contrast, Amelia, who loves her child dearly, hands George Jr. over to Mr. Osborne, her father-in-law, who she hopes will give the boy what she cannot—money. The selfless Dobbin again intervenes, however, and convinces old Osborne that little Georgy and Amelia, a sweet lass and a decent mum, need his financial assistance.

With George and Rawdon out of the way, and any semblance of respectability out of the question, Becky sets out to achieve what she had aspired to at the beginning of the story: she aims to win the hand (or maybe just the fortune) of Amelia's brother Joseph. Indeed, she manages to get all of his money before he dies. Did she . . . murder him? Alas, that's an answer neither Becky, nor Thackeray, ever provides, but Becky does give Amelia the inside scoop on her late husband George. Amelia now feels free to marry Dobbin and does so.

ALL IS VANITY

In *Vanity Fair* Thackeray remade the novel of manners, transforming it even more than Jane Austen had done. You might say she passed him the torch. What Austen set out to do in village England, Thackeray accomplished on a broader scale. It's true that *Vanity Fair* sprawls over a broad canvas of characters and events, but what vivid scenes he gives us, like the chaos in Brussels at the Battle of Waterloo. (He was a journalist, after all.) And what an array of human types! You may not meet his characters every day, but you're bound to meet a "user" like Becky Sharp at least once in your life.

As a satirist, Thackeray exposed sham, pretense, and self-deception. Isn't that what Tom Wolfe did in *Bonfire of the Vanities,* and where do you think he got his title?

THOMAS BABINGTON MACAULAY (1800–1859)

Thomas Babington Macaulay (1800–1859).

Macaulay, a contemporary of Thackeray, was a statesman, historian, biographer, and essayist. Thackeray knew him primarily for his essays and reviews, published in his *Critical and Historical Essays.* Macaulay is best known for his *History of England from the Accession of James the Second.* By modern standards he's not the most readable author, but his account of the great fire of London was a Victorian bestseller.

If you find it hard keeping up with all the walk-on parts in this novel, think of what it must have been like to be responsible for them. *Vanity Fair*'s got plenty of problems with "continuity," as they call it in the moving picture industry. Characters mysteriously change names, and chronology goes out the window.

In another sense, however, there's too much continuity—that is, the characters never evolve, as real people do. Becky's always on the make, and Amelia's always slow on the uptake, and Dobbin, the noblest character in the book, is unflaggingly devoted. Only drastic events like the onset of poverty or a great battle alter the course of their lives. Amelia does not abandon her fond memories of her louse of a husband until Becky thrusts the proof of his bad behavior in her face.

Quite a few critics have condemned Thackeray's art for adopting the same *Vanity Fair* values he condemns. Except for Becky Sharp, his characters are flat, one-dimensional, and, as people, are no more real than the hollow principles they live by. Well, it's true that he doesn't render an accurate psychological portrait of his characters the way Charlotte Brontë did, but that doesn't mean that types like Becky Sharp don't exist in the real world. Thackeray's concern is to hold up for criticism the sort of society that produces a Becky Sharp.

POST-*VANITY*

Vanity Fair made his reputation, but the 1848 publication of *The Book of Snobs* helped solidify it. These were collected satires Thackeray published while he worked at *Punch*, a satirical magazine.

He confirmed his genius with *Pendennis, Henry Esmond,* and its sequel, *The Virginians.* There's also *The Memoirs of Barry Lyndon*, which was later made into a movie with Marisa Berenson. In 1862, he gave up editorship of *Cornhill Magazine* because he didn't like returning rejection slips. Shortly before Thackeray died in 1863, he made up with Dickens, with whom he had been feuding since 1858.

JUST FOR LAUGHS

Punch is an illustrated weekly comic periodical first published in 1841. Joseph Last was its first printer, and the cartoonist George Cruikshank did the original illustrations. Cruikshank had won fame for his sketches for Dickens's early novels, *Oliver Twist* in particular (he said that he used himself as his model for the character Fagin). Later Sir John Tenniel, best known for his illustrations for Lewis Carroll's *Alice in Wonderland,* was a frequent contributor to *Punch,* as was Thackery, whose most famous contribution was his seven parodies of contemporary novelists which included a satire of the works of the American novelist James Fenimore Cooper. The figure of Punch and the dog Toby appeared on the cover from the first issue to 1969.

S U M M A R Y

 He was the only novelist who could compete with Charles Dickens for the title of England's most popular writer.

 He lost his inheritance gambling, so he gambled on a career as an author.

 His most famous character, Becky Sharp, is synonymous with a scheming, manipulative woman, the predecessor of Scarlett O'Hara in *Gone With the Wind.*

 He exposed hypocrisy, pretense, and class distinction.

CHAPTER 6

ANTHONY TROLLOPE

(1815–1882)

YOU MUST REMEMBER THIS

The Barsetshire novels are Trollope's main contribution to literature. These are gems of character, milieu, and satire—okay, so plot wasn't his forte. You want everything?

MOST FAMOUS FOR

Writing 47 novels, which is more than anyone but a dogged and dateless Ph.D. candidate could— or would—read. Here are the ones you should try:

- ★ *The Warden* (1855)
- ★ *Doctor Thorne* (1858)
- ★ *Barchester Towers* (1857)
- ★ *Framley Parsonage* (1861)
- ★ *The Last Chronicle of Barset* (1867)

IT'S A FAMILY AFFAIR

Though Anthony Trollope's father was a barrister—not a bad way to make a living in Victorian England—he was not one to sweat the details: Trollope Sr. had a penchant for bizarre get-rich-quick schemes, of the Ginzu knife/Florida swampland variety. As a result, Anthony's family teetered on the brink of bankruptcy for most of Trollope's childhood, avoiding disgrace only through the efforts of his mother, Fanny Trollope. One of Mr. Trollope's strangest schemes involved setting up a giant Trump-like bazaar in Cincinnati, Ohio, USA. He sent Fanny to supervise the building of this monstrosity, but funds were exhausted before the place could be stocked. Deciding it would be easier to write novels to support her family than do anything else, Fanny embarked on a remarkable literary career. When her husband finally went bankrupt in 1834, she grabbed her kids and penniless mate and split to Belgium, where she kept churning out the novels—forty-one in all.

Fanny Trollope (1780–1863). Novelist, travel writer, mom.

Taking a page from his mother's book, Anthony eventually turned to writing novels to make money and was equally successful. But there were additional reasons for his taking up the quill, and since we've all read Freud, we'll blame it on his early years. Anthony had a truly wretched childhood. When he was seven, he went to Harrow as a day student.

THE LITERARY CAREER OF FANNY TROLLOPE (1771–1863)

Nearly as prolific an author as her famous son Anthony, Fanny Trollope wrote her first book at the age of fifty-seven. Titled *Domestic Manners of the Americans* (1828), her literary debut—a chronicle of her four years in America—was a best-seller but hardly a tribute to her host country. She angered critics with her attack on American slavery, subjugation of women, and what she considered the course personal habits of Midwest merchant farmers and Mississippi River squatters. Yet the book sold so well that the money it earned saved the Trollope family from financial ruin. Her novels reflect her gift for satire and her strong sense of social justice, as in *The Life and Adventures of Michael Armstrong, The Factory Boy* (1830), which exposes the exploitation of factory workers. Her other novels, notably *Second Love* (1851), *Mrs. Matthews* (1851), and *Uncle Walter* (1852), championed the cause of women trapped in unhappy marriages.

A very poor boy among the very rich boys, he was utterly miserable. When the money was exhausted, the family moved him to another school, Winchester, but he was forced to leave there as well because of unpaid tuition. Hoping that the past was all a dream, Mr. Trollope tried Harrow again, but the boys remembered Anthony's poverty and were terribly cruel. Anthony lived in a run-down farmhouse with his father—his mother was in America—and tramped through the mud twice a day to sit next to children who tipped more for a meal than Anthony's father earned in a week. "Something of the

A HARROWING EXPERIENCE

Founded in 1571 by John Lyon, Harrow was originally chartered to educate the poor boys of the Harrow parish. Fifty years later the school ran into financial difficulties and began accepting paying customers. That was the end of the beginning: from then on, Harrow became one of the most prestigious, elite, "public" (meaning private) schools in England. Graduates include the English statesmen Sir Robert Peel, Lord Palmerston, and Winston Churchill; Irish dramatist Richard Brinsley Sheridan; and the poet Lord Byron. The closest American equivalents are Philips Exeter Academy, Groton, and Choate.

Harrow, Middlesex County—proving ground for England's young elite.

disgrace of my schooldays clung to me all through life," he later wrote.

When Anthony was nineteen, the family pulled some strings and got him a post office job, at which Anthony was astonishingly inept. He was unpunctual, insubordinate, and forever in trouble. On one particular day a woman sailed into the office screaming, "Anthony Trollope, when are you going to marry my daughter?" He did not have to marry the young woman, but he was not recommended for regular merit raises, either. The post office and Anthony Trollope endured each other for seven years, until his supervisor recommended him for a job in Ireland, as probably the best available way to be rid of him.

Ireland worked a transformation on Trollope. For the first time he made some friends, and there is no record of any other indignant mothers demanding that he do right by their daughters. He traveled a great deal, through England, Egypt, America, and the West Indies. With his newfound happiness came the urge to write, and at the age of forty, he published his first novel, *The Warden*. Suddenly, he had everything he had always wanted: respect, friendship, success. Divinely happy, Trollope thoroughly enjoyed his new life. He was laughing when he had a stroke and died at the age of sixty-seven.

THE BARSETSHIRE SERIES

At first, Trollope tried to give readers what they had

IRELAND

Ireland, the second largest island of the British Isles, is now divided into Northern Ireland, a constituent part of Great Britain, and the Republic of Ireland, formerly Eire. Trollope was in Ireland during the disastrous potato famine (1845–1847). He also witnessed the beginning of agitation for home rule. Today, aside from warm thick beer, forty shades of green, and the value added tax, Ireland is venerated among writers and other creative types as a tax haven.

Ireland's poor at the workhouse gate during the potato famine of 1845–1847.

come to expect—realism, a slice of life faithfully re-
corded and pleasantly related. It didn't work; the early
books were mutts. It was only when he dropped the slice-
of-life routine and went for the hazy impression-of-life
that the pieces fell into place. *The Warden* is a record of
the villages and towns, churches and homes, clergy and
laity, and manners and social life of his age filtered

WHO'S
H
O
☞

The Warden:
A LITERARY TOUT SHEET

The Reverend Septimus Harding: The lights
are on and no one's home: the befuddled but
nonetheless amiable singing master of Barchester Cathedral and warden (administrator) of
Hiram's Hospital.

Eleanor Harding: His clever daughter.

John Bold: Her lover.

Dr. Grantly: The husband of Mr. Harding's
elder daughter; destined to become a regular
in the Barchester sitcom.

Tom Towers: Golly, Mr. Kent: the Jimmy Olsen
of the newspaper world.

Sir Abraham Haphazard: Mr. Harding's legal
beagle.

through his imagination. It was the first of the six novels in the Barsetshire series.

LIFE AMONG THE INMATES

The Warden

At age fifty, the Reverend Septimus Harding is appointed precentor of Barchester Cathedral. For the one or two of you who are not intimately versed in ecclesiastical life during Victoria's reign, a precentor is a singing master for a church choir. Along with trilling his gills, the Reverend Harding received the wardenship of Hiram's Hospital, an old-age charity home for the not-so-dirty dozen. This is a cushy sinecure: since the Hospital is over four hundred years old, the endowment is as big as the GNP of a small banana republic, and the warden gets a hefty pile of bananas. With this income of eight hundred pounds a year, Harding can keep his daughter Eleanor happy. He does not have to worry about his older daughter, Susan, who is married to Dr. Grantly, the cranky archdeacon of the cathedral.

John Bold, a physician with too much time on his hands, decides that Reverend Harding is overpaid. He agitates the inmates and involves Tom Towers, the newspaperman. Harding is so upset by Tower's editorials in the *Jupiter* that he contemplates resigning and taking up residence in Crabtree Parva, a small parish that pays £50 a year. But Grantly will not hear of Harding leaving and tries to sway the inmates. His efforts prove in vain. It's time for Grantly to bring in the big gun—Harding's daughter Eleanor.

She visits John Bold and begs him to drop his suit. In

IT'S A LIVING

During this time, it was in the power of important families to decide the appointments (livings) of the parishes around their estates. These livings guaranteed to their lucky recipients a fixed amount of property or income without requiring a fixed amount of work. Holding a living was not the same as working—the recipient had few real responsibilities, the actual work being carried out by underlings.

Today we admire those who work for a living, but among the upper classes in nineteenth-century England, "trade"—what we would today call business and commerce—was looked upon as being beneath the dignity of cultivated people. To spend one's time in the avid pursuit of money—profit—was considered vulgar. Business was not the traditional occupation of the great families of England, who derived their incomes from the possession of land. So call us vulgar; it's all the Puritans' fault for bringing over the Protestant work ethic.

time-honored fashion, he offers her a trade: he will drop the suit if she will be his one and only. They immediately declare their love for each other.

Deciding that he can no longer accept the overly-large income, Harding goes to London to confer with Sir Abraham Haphazard, counsel for the defense. He tells Sir Abraham that he must in all conscience resign; back in Barchester, he tenders his resignation to the bishop. Harding accepts the living at a small parish, Eleanor marries John Bold, Harding keeps his cello at Eleanor's, and all's well that ends well.

PLOT, PLOT, WHO'S GOT THE PLOT?

The Warden

You might have noticed that something was missing in the well-crafted description you just read: a plot. *The Warden* is typical of all of Trollope's novels in its blatant disregard for plot. Trollope did not have an aversion to plots; on the contrary, he felt they were very nice things, but just not for him. Rather, he was concerned with describing moral character. Archdeacon Grantly and his father-in-law, Septimus Harding, so fascinated Trollope that they reappear in his novels and serve as moral touchstones. Harding was at the upper range of goodness, a gentle man devoted to his cello and the music in his cathedral. The archdeacon was more worldly and ambitious. Further, you will notice that there is no villain in this novel, nor any burning social issue: Trollope started with the hardly earth-shattering problem of how to best use the church endowment.

LIFE IN THE COUNTRY

Barchester Towers

Bishop Grantly of Barchester has gone to meet his Maker, which leaves a nice corner office vacant. His bishop's son, the archdeacon, hopes for the key to the executive washroom, but the coveted prize goes to Dr. Proudie instead. The power behind the throne is Mrs. Proudie, Attila the Hun in drag. She keeps her man, the parish, and his assistant, the odious Obidiah Slope, firmly under her heel. Now here's where it gets rough: keep in mind that Trollope's not a big man on plot.

WHO'S WHO ☞

Barchester Towers:
A LITERARY TOUT SHEET

Bishop Proudie: Bishop of Barchester, a hen-pecked wonder.

Mrs. Proudie: The missus; just a heartbeat away from the Bishop's seat, but since no one told her, she's busy running the show.

The Reverend Obadiah Slope: The Bishop's chaplain, so odious that he makes Tiny Tim and his ukulele look like a Chippendale dancer.

The Reverend Septimus Harding: Excuse me, but haven't we met before? Yes! You met him in *The Warden*.

Mrs. Eleanor Bold: Are you detecting a pattern here? (from *The Warden*)

Dr. Grantley: The Archdeacon of Barchester, who was last seen in *The Warden*.

Charlotte Stanhope: Mrs. Bold's friend; a new character.

La Signora Madeline Vesey Neroni, née Stanhope: Charlotte's sister; would spend her days watching television if it had been invented.

Ethelbert   Stanhope   (Bertie):   Charlotte's

WHO'S
WHO ☞

(*continued*)

brother, into conspicuous consumption, charging to the max, and changing religions.

Mr. Quiverful: Mrs. Proudie's candidate for warden of Hiram's Hospital; the gentleman has fourteen children so we know what his quiver is full of . . .

The Reverend Francis Arabin: Dean of the cathedral.

On the first Sunday of the new bishop's leadership, the Reverend Slope holds sway. He speaks on the importance of simplicity in the church service. To implement his words, he's decided to abolish chanting, intoning, and formal ritual. This does not go over well with the masses; as a matter of fact, they are utterly aghast. For generations the service has been chanted; if it ain't broke, why fix it? It is decided that the Reverend Slope will never darken the pulpit again. What to do to pass the time? He stirs up a little trouble.

Through Slope, the bishop announces that absentee clergymen should return and help run the diocese. For years, Dr. Stanhope has left his chores to his curates while he soaked up the sun and spaghetti in Italy; no fool he. So Stanhope returns, trailed by his ailing wife and three grown children: spinster Charlotte, exotic La Signora Madeline Vesey Neroni, and ne'er-do-well Ethel-

MOVING ON UP IN THE WORLD OF GOD

Since *The Occupational Handbook* does not list the hierarchy of religious slots, and in this tight job market you might be inclined to give the religious life a whirl, here's a quick crib. (NB: It helps if you have a modicum of faith, or pretense thereof. It's also a good idea to be some variety of Christian.)

- "Arch" means chief, so the Archbishop is the chief officer of an archdiocese or archbishopric. This is a tough job to get your first time out. We suggest you start a little further down on the list.
- Bishops oversee a number of local churches or a diocese. Bishops tend to be career men, managing the shop rather than leading the flock.
- Rectors are clergymen in charge of a parish.
- Curates assist rectors or vicars. Good entry-level slot.

bert. La Signora is one of the world's first couch potatoes; Bertie tries on religions as other men do neckties.

Meanwhile, on the marriage front, we have Eleanor Bold, a widow with a small child and a comfortable income. Attention fortune hunters: hot prospect ahead. Ambitious Obadiah needs no such road sign: he knows a good thing when he sees one. Eleanor detests Slope, partly because she can recognize a creep but also because he has put the screws to her gentle, sweet father. The Stanhope sisters also have their eye on Eleanor for their brother Bertie.

Soon after, Eleanor finds herself in a carriage with Slope. He seizes the opportunity to embrace her and declare his love. Finding this about as appealing as two weeks in Trenton, she tells him where he can put his arm and his affections. Bertie, a master of diplomacy, tells Eleanor that his sisters have urged him to marry her for her money. When Dr. Stanhope learns what an idiot his son has been, he sends him away to earn his own living and find still another religion.

Slope is sent off to another diocese, the Stanhopes scoot back to Italy, and Eleanor marries Arabin, the dean of the cathedral. Everyone gets his or her just deserts and the reader has a hoot.

POLITICAL DOINGS

The Barsetshire novels are most often regarded as Trollope's chief—if not only—qualification for literary immortality. They hold this position because of their wonderful characters and setting, but also because they are a gosh-darned good read. Trollope's strength as a novelist lay in his ability to describe the manners and morals of the world he was anxious to join. Despite his affection for his characters, he could not resist the chance to satirize their foibles. Reading one of the Barsetshire novels is like a month in the country, the country as it was before your neighbor got the chain saw and started defoliating Walden Pond. "Barset," J. B. Priestley has commented, "is a haven of rest."

But we would not be bothering to write this essay if that's all there was to the Barsetshire series. Trollope's more solid qualities are evident in much of his other work (and there certainly is much more to consider), where his imagination can be revealed to greater depth.

This depth is especially evident in the political novels whose central characters are Plantagenet Palliser and his

J. B. PRIESTLEY

J. B. Priestley (1894–1984).

John Boynton Priestley, an English writer, excelled in a number of genres. A newspaper essayist and critic, he regularly inveighed against materialism and mechanization in society in *The New Statesman* and *The Nation*. Two novels, *The Good Companions* (1929) and *Angel Pavement* (1930), established him in that genre as well. His plays, especially *Dangerous Corner* (1932), *An Inspector Calls* (1946), and *Dragon's Mouth* (1952) were experimental in form. He also wrote studies of England. Don't confuse him with Joseph Priestley (1733–1804), the British chemist who isolated and described several gases, including oxygen. The first was full of hot air; the second tried to find it.

wife Glencora: *Can You Forgive Her?* (1864-65), *Phineas Finn* (1869), *The Eustace Diamonds* (1873), *Phineas Redux* (1874), *The Prime Minister* (1876), and *The Duke's Children* (1880).

The milieu is now London and the main characters are people of wealth and status. As in the earlier series, these books are as crowded as a trendy singles joint on a Friday night. Further, Trollope's characters are moved by the forces that animate a certain few of today's unattached: love and property. Plantagenet Palliser is a much more complex character than any we have encountered before in a Trollope novel. This complexity allows Trollope to delve into the political doings of his day. Trollope himself was a Liberal, with touches of Tory in his temperament. He was in favor of the spread of democracy and education. Palliser is a Whig, a man of wealth and title, with liberal leanings.

THE PLANTAGENETS

The Plantagenets were a dynasty of English kings from Henry II (1154) to the ascension of the Tudors in 1485. Trollope uses the name Plantagenet as a satirical reference to the ambitions of the Pallisers to achieve political power. Plantagenet Palliser finally becomes a duke and a prime minister, but never quite makes it to king.

Whether you read the Barsetshire series or Trollope's more political Palliser novels, you're in for a treat. Grab a Trollope novel, a blanket, and some sunblock and head for the beach. We guarantee a great afternoon.

Cartoonist Frederick Waddy's portrait of Trollope, 1872.

SUMMARY

⏱ Wrote hilarious, insightful sketches of clerical life that made him one of the leading humorous commentators on Victorian society.

⏱ Turned out forty-seven novels, before the days of word processors and computers.

⏱ Has kept the BBC and PBS in plots for years.

GEORGE ELIOT
(1819–1880)

GEORGE ELIOT: A ROSE
BY ANY OTHER NAME . . .

L et's start with the name game. George Eliot was the pseudonym of Marian Evans. We shall refer to the author by her real name, Evans, until we get to the part where her name began to wear pants, so to speak. But that's just the beginning. Marian was also known as Mary Ann to her family. A young friend called her Clematis; her mentor, Deutera. She signed her letters Mrs. Lewes; her female devotees called her Our Lady. Her adoptive sons referred to her as Mutter; after her death she was celebrated as Mrs. John W. Cross. Got all that? There's going to be a test at the end.

Mary Anne Evans
A.K.A.
George Eliot
A.K.A.
Occupant

Mail

A. BRALL

Fortunately for Evans, her parents kept her names straight and recognized her remarkable intellectual gifts. Her father, a prosperous estate manager, sent Marian to exclusive schools where she learned to speak French fluently and to read Latin, German, and Greek. After her father's death in 1849, Evans became friendly with

GIRLS WILL BE BOYS

Pseudonyms were all the rage in Victorian fiction. Dickens used one for his first few novels—"Boz," a corruption of "Moses," a nickname he gave his younger brother who couldn't pronounce it properly. Women authors, fearful of rejection on the basis of gender, found pen names especially convenient. Besides George Eliot, we have the other "George" in France, the notorious Amandine Dupin, the Baronne Dudevant (1804–1876), who wrote under the name of George Sand. She not only assumed a man's name, but she also dressed in masculine attire and smoked a cigar. In Ireland two women, Violet Martin and Edith Somerville, collaborated on a series of hilarious sketches of country life entitled *Experiences of an Irish R.M.* (1899), under the assumed identities of Martin Ross and E.O. Somerville. And of course we have the Brontës fooling everyone with their androgynous monikers, Acton, Currer, and Ellis Bell—their own father never even suspected that his daughters were authors.

the freethinking philosophers Charles Henell and Charles and Caroline Bray. Bray was the author of *The Philosophy of Necessity*, a philosophical inquiry into the nature of man. Caroline had no objections to Evans' obvious infatuation with her husband, because everyone knew he was already friendly with their cook, who bore him six children, and thus gave added resonance to that well-worn euphemism, "a bun in the oven." Under Bray's influence, Evans cast off formal religion and realized that there was more to life than studying German and thinking of great pen names.

PHRENOLOGY: BUMP AND GRIND

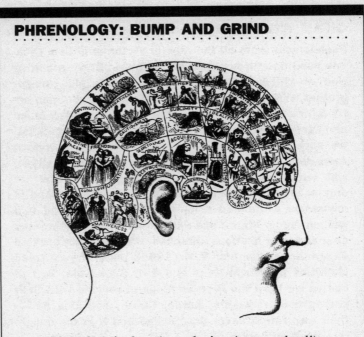

Phrenologist's chart (now that's using your head!).

Evans attended Bray's classes in phrenology, the pseudoscience in which character analysis was based on the physical characteristics of the skull. Phrenologists made the reasonable assumption that specific parts of the body and brain were linked. From this came the witless conclusion that abstract qualities like integrity or depravity were similarly localized and revealed through the bumps and ridges of the skull. Although this notion was rejected by many scientists of the time, a number of journals were devoted to the technique of reading a patient's head as if it were a road map.

In 1851, Evans moved to London and plunged into the world of letters. Her brilliant mind and deep learning snared her the coveted position of assistant editor for the *Westminster Review*. Evans hobnobbed with such eminent Victorians as philosopher Herbert Spencer, writer Charles Dickens, and John Stuart Mill, a Big Man on Campus if ever there was one.

JOHN STUART MILL: B.M.O.C.

John Stuart Mill (1806–1873).

John Stuart Mill (1806–1873) had an enormous influence on the intellectual history of his century. Primarily concerned with protecting individualism in a democracy, Mills worked to prove that people are more important than institutions that govern them, such as the church or state. Must Read: *On Liberty* (1859).

Evans and Spencer became friends, but apparently Evans wanted more than companionship and defied the conventions of romance by proposing marriage to him. Spencer was horrified—like most Englishmen of his day he would have considered it unusually assertive for a woman to read books, never mind propose marriage. He was also put off by her plain face, straightforward nature, and dowdy clothes. Evans's keen mind might have made her an engaging acquaintance, but the implication is that Herbert preferred lovers who were cute and mute.

The man who became Marian Evans's boon companion was George Henry Lewes, drama critic for *The*

George Henry Lewes (1817– 1878). Marian Evans's common-law husband, George Eliot's biggest fan.

Leader. Lewes was eccentric: one of his favorite pastimes was to accost famous actors and authors by introducing himself as someone they should know. He also liked to shock Victorian matrons with the intimate details of his sexual adventures. At first, Evans was put off by Lewes's manner. The fact that he was married might also have contributed to her hesitation. But he was soon separated from his wife, whose ongoing liaison with T. L. Hunt produced four children. Six months later Evans and Lewes were an item.

Evans eventually moved in with Lewes and became his common-law wife. When society and Evans's own brother shunned the couple, they went off to the Continent. Despite their isolation, the liaison was happy and intellectually productive: Lewes was the one who encouraged Evans to write a series of stories and submit them under a masculine pseudonym, an obligatory ruse for most nineteenth-century female writers in England. Honoring Evans's change of name, we'll call her George Eliot from now on.

The success of the stories encouraged Eliot to write her first novel, *Adam Bede* (1859). The novel was welcomed with great critical acclaim and Eliot entered the exalted ranks of major novelists such as Dickens and Thackeray. Few of the literary cognoscenti had a clue to the author's identity and so she escaped whipping as "an immoral woman." No such luck the second time around when Eliot's true identity as a woman was revealed: *The Mill on the Floss* was condemned because Eliot's sex and

THE WOMAN QUESTION

"Why can't a woman be more like a man?" moaned Henry Higgins as he attempted to teach Eliza Doolittle to talk like a lady. Henry wasn't the first to have problems with the ladies: the Victorians pondered the relationship between men and women ad nauseam. It was generally accepted that men were smarter than women; a respected guidebook assured readers that "the Average Weight of Man's Brain is 3½ lbs.; Woman's 2 lbs., 11 oz." The alternate conclusion, that men just might be fatheads, did not occur to the scientists of the day.

Queen Victoria (1819–1901). Ruled Great Britain from 1837–1901, yet dismissed the idea of women's suffrage as "this mad folly."

Even Queen Victoria entered the fray. On one hand, she believed that women should be educated, and helped establish a college for women in 1847. On the other hand, she campaigned against giving women the vote, which she called "this mad folly." A concerned (male) citizen warned, "grant suffrage to women, and you will have to build insane asylums in every county, and establish a divorce court in every town. Women are too nervous and hysterical to enter into politics."

In those days, women were cherished for their tenderness, innocence, affection, and submissiveness. Promiscuity, dancing in hot rooms, too much reading, and the attentions of an overly-romantic husband could send the frail sex into a swoon.

Middlemarch:
A LITERARY TOUT SHEET

Dorothea Brooke: Our Miss Brooke is the heroine of the novel. Her only flaw, like her creator's, is an annoying tendency to change names. In case it comes up at your next cocktail party, she becomes Mrs. Casaubon and then Mrs. Ladislaw.

Celia Brooke: Dorothea's younger sister, who marries Sir James Chettam, her sister's leftover beau.

Arthur Brooke: Dorothea and Celia's uncle, symbol of The English Squire.

The Reverend Edward Casaubon: Dorothea's first husband, a pedantic snooze.

Will Ladislaw: Dorothea's second husband, a young and handsome dude whose literary and artistic talents make him suspect to the people of Middlemarch.

Dr. Tertius Lydgate: The novel's hero, a physician whose ideals are crushed by the reality of marriage to shop-till-you-drop Rosamund.

Rosamund Vincy: The beautiful selfish deb who marries Dr. Lydgate.

(*continued*)

Fred Vincy: Rosamund's younger brother who spends himself into a hole, which prevents him from marrying his love, Mary Garth.

Mary Garth: Salt-of-the-earth daughter of the estate agent who insists that her fiancé Fred get his head on straight before they marry.

her out-of-wedlock living arrangements had become known. Regardless of such condemnation, Eliot was firmly established as a principal figure in English literature with the publication of *Silas Marner* in 1861. *Middlemarch*, generally regarded as her masterpiece, appeared serially in eight parts from 1871 to 72. The story so hooked its audience that even such a sophisticated reader as Eliot's publisher, John Blackwood, begged advance copies of the chapters because he couldn't wait for the next installment.

George Lewes died in 1878, but his bereaved widow found comfort in the arms of her financial advisor, John Walter Cross. Though Eliot was over sixty and her new man twenty years her junior, their 1880 marriage seemed to be a happy occasion. Cross marked their honeymoon in Venice by falling accidentally from a hotel window into the Grand Canal, where he was fished out by the gondoliers. Cross survived, though wet behind the ears, but his bride died of heart failure seven months later.

MIDDLEMARCH: WHERE THERE'S A WILL, THERE'S A WAY

Middlemarch centers on Dorothea Brooke. Unlike her pretty sister Celia, Dorothea is highly intelligent and seeks an intellectual partner in marriage. But love is nearsighted, and Dorothea makes the mistake of choosing Edward Casaubon, a clergyman thirty years her senior. She finds to her dismay that he is pretentious, dull, and critical, not to mention seriously *old*. Even a sponge bath seems out of reach insofar as shared sensuality is concerned.

Dorothea meets her husband's young cousin, Will Ladislaw, and the sizzle starts. Consumed with jealousy, Edward attaches a codicil to his will to cut off Dorothea's income if she marries Ladislaw. Edward dies of a heart attack, and Dorothea rejects her legacy to marry Will.

The book also concerns the beautiful but self-centered Rosamund Vincy, who marries Dr. Tertius Lydgate. Rosamund's extravagance plunges Lydgate into debt and he neglects his medical practice. He dies at age fifty, his illusions about marriage shattered.

The novel's third romance ends happily. Rosamund's foolish brother Fred Vincy and his sensible sweetheart Mary Garth sink into a slough of marital bliss after Mary obliges Fred to face reality, pay his debts, and get a job as an estate manager. So what does it all mean? If that were your "30-point interpretation" question, this would be a reasonable answer:

The novel is a rejection of the false values of money, class, and power. Dorothea, in sacrificing her legacy, gains the love of a worthy man, Will Ladislaw; Lydgate unhappily discovers that underneath his wife's vapid exterior lies a vapid interior; and Fred Vincy achieves self-respect through the dignity of work. The novel can also be read as social satire of the class system around which English country life revolved. When Dorothea gives up her money to marry Ladislaw, her family and friends recoil in horror. Rosamund Lydgate's refusal to economize in the face of adversity is prompted by her desire to maintain an affluent image. After Lydgate dies, Rosamund becomes a highly respected matron by marrying a wealthy, elderly physician.

ELIOT'S REPUTATION

Contemporary writer Emily Dickinson considered Eliot's achievement in *Middlemarch* to be nothing short of monumental. "What do I think of *Middlemarch*?" she wrote. "What do I think of glory?" After Eliot's death, however, her reputation faded. Subsequent generations consider her work too moralistic, didactic, discursive. Nevertheless, such diverse writers as Henry James, D. H. Lawrence, and Margaret Drabble have acknowledged their debt to her.

THREE OTHER NOVELS
YOU SHOULD KNOW

SILAS MARNER: SOLITARY SILAS

Silas Marner is movie-of-the-week material. Godfrey Cass, the eldest son of the village squire, is being blackmailed

TIME LINE

Here's some trivia from the age of George Eliot, just in case you're finally picked to be on "Jeopardy":

1844	George Williams founds the YMCA; Samuel Morse patents the telegraph
1845	Irish potato famine begins
1848	Marx and Engels publish the Communist Manifesto
1861	America's Civil War begins
1865	Lewis Carroll publishes *Alice in Wonderland*
1869	Suez Canal finished
1876	Alexander Graham Bell patents the telephone
1877	Thomas Edison patents the phonograph
1880	First electric lighting installed
1886	English Lawn Tennis Association founded at Wimbledon
1888	Jack the Ripper stalks London
1898	The Curies discover radium

by his villainous brother, Dunstan, who knows about Godfrey's secret marriage to the drug-addicted barmaid, Molly Farren. If the Squire finds out, Godfrey will be disinherited and will lose his new squeeze, the pretty and respectable Nancy Lammeter. But lucky for Godfrey, Molly never makes it to the Squire's house. She dies in a snowstorm, and her child wanders into the cottage of a lonely weaver, Silas Marner. Molly's death frees Godfrey to marry Nancy Lammeter. Meanwhile, Marner raises the little girl, Eppie, as his own. Sixteen years later, Godfrey Cass wants to claim his daughter, but she turns her back on him and stays with Marner.

WHO'S WHO

Silas Marner:
A LITERARY TOUT SHEET

Silas Marner: The weaver of Raveloe. Concerning his intelligence, it seems as though the elevator doesn't go to the top floor. Actually, he's not so much slow as he is isolated and methodical. Weaving will do that to you.

Godfrey Cass: Originally a profligate gadabout, the love of a good woman encourages him to settle down, and he comes to see that he has been a naughty boy.

William Dane: Steals, slanders, and shatters the life of his friend and fellow weaver, Silas.

Nancy Lammeter: Dignified, reserved, beautiful, loving, and best of all, a meticulous housekeeper. The good woman whom Godfrey marries.

Squire Cass: A caricature of the big fish in a little pond. His success derives more from his heredity, wealth, and name than his own accomplishments.

Eppie: Godfrey Cass's daughter from his first marriage to Molly Farren, she remains loyal to Silas Marner when Daddy Dearest finally acknowledges his paternity.

Priscilla Lammeter: Plain, shrewd, and direct. Sounds a lot like the author to us.

Underneath all this melodrama is an allegory about the double metamorphosis of man. The novel is built on the simple change from faith to loss of faith to regaining faith. Eliot traces how time, nature, and people can remedy a damaged personality. The theme's a swipe from the Romantic poet William Wordsworth, who believed that children bring "hope and forward-looking thoughts." Silas Marner regains a hopeful life through the love he shares with the child Eppie.

ROMANTICISM: EVERYONE LOVES A LOVER

Don't confuse "romance" with the Romantics. The former involves flowers, chocolate, and diamond tennis bracelets; the latter, imagination, freedom, emotion, wildness, the rights of the individual, the nobility of the common person, and the appeal of pastoral life. Romance occurs on Saturday nights in trendy Italian bistros or the back seat of late-model cars; Romanticism is the writings of Wordsworth, Coleridge, Shelley, Keats, and Byron. In her look back to a simpler age, Eliot was right up there with the players. She best exemplifies the Romantics' concern with God, duty, responsibility, and righteousness.

Adam Bede

Adam Bede, a young carpenter, falls in love with pretty but shallow Hetty Sorrell, against his mother's wishes. Hetty has eyes only for Captain Arthur Donnithorne, Adam's friend. Donnithorne seduces Hetty and then leaves to join his regiment. Pretty convenient, we say.

WHO'S WHO ☞

Adam Bede:
A LITERARY TOUT SHEET

Adam Bede: Stern, moralistic village carpenter. The strong, silent type.

Hetty Sorrell: Farmer's niece, young, pretty, self-centered; all the vanity of Madonna, twice the attitude.

Arthur Donnithorne: Young squire whom Hetty pegs as her ticket to Easy Street. Turns out to be a world-class cad.

Dinah Moore: Methodist preacher in love with Adam. Possessed of profound inner calm and strength, devoutly religious. The anti-Hetty.

Martin Poyser: Farmer, uncle to Hetty. Everybody's pal.

Mrs. Poyser: Martin's wife. Victim of verbal diarrhea.

Seth Bede: Adam's kinder, gentler brother. In love with Dinah.

Mr. Irwine: Kindly village vicar.

Bartle Massey: Schoolmaster with a tongue that cuts like a knife.

Hetty, pregnant with Donnithorne's child, agrees to marry Adam but runs away to find Donnithorne. She finally reaches Windsor where Donnithorne is stationed, but finds he has flown the coop to Ireland. She has the baby but terrified, Hetty wanders into the woods and leaves the baby to die.

Hetty is arrested for the murder of her child and sentenced to death. In the nick of time, Donnithorne returns from Ireland and obtains a reprieve for her. Hetty's sentence is commuted to deportation, not such a terrible thing unless you're attached to England's warm beer, constant drizzle, and deep-fried fish parts. Sorrell dies a few years later. And what of the character who gave his name to the novel, you may ask? Bede realizes that he loves the Methodist preacher Dinah Moore, and the two are married.

REALISM

In Chapter 17 of *Adam Bede*, Eliot suspends the plot to set forth her aim as a novelist, which is "the faithful representing of commonplace things, of things as they are, not as they never have been and never will be." On the surface, *Adam Bede* seems to describe a conventional love triangle, set in the country. But it lacks the fairy-tale quality of many Victorian novels. No prince will ever come, and no one is going to live happily ever after. So what is this novel's point?

Adam Bede is a searching examination of the grounds of conduct. There are various love affairs, but the book is not a love story. We do not especially care who marries

---

THE VICTORIA IN VICTORIAN ENGLAND

Why did Queen Victoria's name become synonymous with nineteenth-century England? Why don't we call it "Gladstonian England" after the skilled Liberal leader, or "Disraeli England" for the great Conservative prime minister? First, Victoria held the reins of power longer than any other modern monarch—sixty-four years, to be exact. Second, under her rule, Great Britain came to symbolize the stability, prosperity, and optimism of the age. Also, Victoria restored a sense of decorum and modesty—even prudishness—to a country embarrassed by the scandalous behavior of George III's sons. For these accomplishments, she aroused in the British people deep feelings of affection and admiration.

---

whom, or even if they marry at all. The main source of our interest is in problems of conduct. The characters are *not* trying to live up to an accepted code or find out how to apply standards. Rather, they are trying to discover what standard is valid for them.

Old-fashioned criticism of George Eliot praised the pastoral charm of her early novels and condemned the intellectuality of the later; our judgment today roughly reverses the allotment of praise and blame. With this shift has come a revival of interest in Eliot, especially in such pastoral novels as *Adam Bede.*

The Mill on the Floss

The plot revolves around the relationship of Maggie Tulliver and her unfeeling brother Tom. Maggie is caught in a compromising situation with her cousin

Lucy's fiancé, Stephen Guest. Tom harshly judges her ostensibly immoral conduct. Despite his condemnation, Maggie's love for her brother is so great that she sacrifices her life to save him in a flood that courses through the town. Both siblings drown, but just before they are swept into the whirlpool, they reconcile.

WHO'S HO

The Mill on the Floss:
A LITERARY TOUT SHEET

Maggie Tulliver: Strong-willed, precocious, high-strung heroine. A misfit and a loner as a child (though fiercely loyal to her brother Tom), she grows up into a jet-haired beauty admired by all—that is, until she is dishonored and ostracized once again.

Tom Tulliver: Maggie's brother and object of her devotion. Dull, narrow-minded, uncompromising. A control freak.

Mr. Tulliver: Miller of Dorlcote Mill on the river Floss, father of Maggie and Tom. Stubborn and ignorant, but warmhearted and sincere. Mistrusts lawyers and other smooth-talkers.

Mrs. Tulliver: Status-conscious pedant.

Mrs. Glegg, Mrs. Deane, and Mrs. Pullett: Mrs. Tulliver's sisters. See above.

**WHO'S
H
O**
☞

(*continued*)

Lucy Deane: Sweet, obedient little doll, complete with blond ringlets and rosy cheeks. Constantly held up as an example to Maggie.

Stephen Guest: Lucy's tall, dark, and handsome fiancé. He falls for Maggie and inadvertently ruins her reputation.

Philip Wakem: Maggie's soulmate. Hunchbacked from birth, his deformity isolates him from the society of the small town, making him a loner like young Maggie. The two find solace in books, intellectual discussion, and, above all, each other's company.

CHARACTERIZATION IN
THE MILL ON THE FLOSS

"There is not a single person in the book of the smallest importance to anybody in the world but themselves, or whose qualities deserved so much as a line of printer's type in their description," fulminated one critic. He was wrong. The source of Eliot's power lies in her steady, realistic eye. To Eliot, the characters she created in *The Mill on the Floss* were valuable precisely because they were typical, because they could stand for others besides themselves. In her characters, Eliot rejected the traditional notion that tragedy had to have a greatness or grandeur to it. Ironically, she created a greatness by awakening her readers' consciousness, enabling them to take the full measure of the situation.

Isaac Evans: Big Brother did not approve of his sister's "alternative" lifestyle.

THE MILL ON THE FLOSS

In life as in literature . . . Tom was modeled on Isaac Evans, Eliot's brother. Although the siblings had been close as children, they grew apart as they matured. After Isaac learned of his sister's liaison with George Lewes, he ordered the family to break off all communication with Eliot. When *The Mill on the Floss* was published, Isaac denied that its author was his sister.

SUMMARY

 Celebrated for her realistic depiction of English village life.

 The novels were set in a rural England whose placid, slow-moving ways would eventually succumb to the rumblings of the Industrial Revolution.

 Created ingenious plot structures, in-depth characterization, and ethical considerations.

 Made it as a woman in a man's world.

CHAPTER 8

RUDYARD KIPLING
(1865–1936)

YOU MUST REMEMBER THIS

Among the Geritol set, Kipling is revered as the tub-thumper for British imperialism, a virtuoso of poetic rhythms, and a short-story writer nonpareil. To the Nintendo generation, he's a star player on the Disney Channel.

MOST FAMOUS FOR

Being the first English author to own an automobile. Incidentally, he was also the first English writer to win the Nobel Prize for Literature (1907). The conventional wisdom is that Kipling is a master of the short story and poetry but can't go the distance in a novel. CW is wrong; the novel *Kim* disproves the rule. Here are some of his famous novels, stories, and poems:

Books

★ *The Man Who Would Be King* (1888)
★ *The Jungle Books* (1894, 1895)
★ *Captains Courageous* (1897)
★ *Kim* (1901)

Poems

★ *The Charge of the Light Brigade*
★ *The White Man's Burden*
★ *The Road to Mandalay*
★ *Gunga Din*
★ *Mowgli's Song Against People*
★ *My Boy Jack*
★ *Danny Deever*
★ *Recessional*
★ *Mandalay*
★ *The Ladies*

"We're Poor Little Lambs Who've Lost Our Way, Baa! Baa! Baa!" This refrain from Kipling's poem *Gentleman Rankers* unfortunately describes Kipling's own childhood. His youth was as wretched as anything out of a Dickens novel, but like too many bad movies, it started out beautifully.

Like his distinguished coeval, Thackeray, Kipling was born in India. Kipling *père* had gone to Bombay to teach at an art school. Neither parent raked in the big bucks, but both enjoyed the privileges and comforts of being members of the "imperial race." Young Rudy had his own ayah, as the Indian nurses were called, and his own manservant. Chief among the customs enjoyed by well-off parents living during the heyday of the British Empire was a limited amount of contact with one's offspring. Hence, Rudy spent his time with his nurse and servant. In fact, he saw his parents so rarely that he spoke Hindi before he knew English.

In 1871, the Kiplings returned to England to see about educating Rudyard and his sister Alice. It was customary for Britons living abroad to return their offspring to the motherland to make sure the children developed the proper stiffness in their upper lips. Besides, life was tough in India—infant mortality was staggering—and little ones can be such a bother. Since the Kiplings seemed sincerely devoted to their children, their action might seem nothing short of inexplicable to us today, were we unaware of the prevailing customs of Kipling's day. Not only did mother and father neglect to tell Rudyard or Alice that the future students had one-way tickets; but the elder Kiplings selected foster parents of

HE AIN'T HEAVY; HE'S MY BROTHER
(OR, THE WHITE MAN'S BURDEN).

Imperialism was in the air; colonies provided raw materials and markets for Britain. Aside from looking good in the accounts books, they made nice vacation spots. But for those not swayed by the profit motive or a week in India's hellish climate, the clincher was Kipling's argument: the English had a responsibility to bring "civilization" to the natives. Kipling called it "the white man's burden." The Empire had two sorts of land: "settled" territories, where whites made up the bulk of the population; and outright colonies, in which few whites lived. The first included Canada, Australia, and New Zealand; the second, Hong Kong and India. In 1856, after the sepoys (Indian troops under British command) rebelled, Britain stopped pussyfooting around, shoved aside the British East India Company, and seized the country outright.

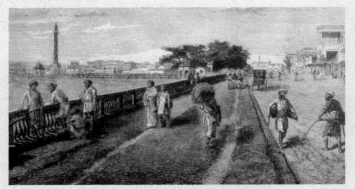

*Calcutta, India, in the days when the
sun never set on the British Empire.*

An allegorical rendering of "Hope" by Sir Edward Burne-Jones (1833–1898), Kipling's kindly uncle.

the kind you see featured on "America's Most Wanted." Rudyard was bullied and beaten by his bitter guardian, "Aunty Rosa," for the next six years. Unsurprisingly, the experience colored Kipling's entire life. Much of his fiction contains descriptions of hallucinations, nightmares, and mental breakdowns; Kipling himself became an insomniac, which would play a key role in his imagination. The child's most important escape was his annual Christmas visit to his aunt and uncle's home, The Grange, in Fulham. Aside from providing a respite from his misery, The Grange hosted some of the brightest stars of the second wave of the "Pre-Raphaelite Movement." Kipling's uncle, Edward Burne-Jones, and other kindly members of the artistic and literary avant-garde exerted a powerful influence on the bereft child.

In 1882, when he was seventeen, Kipling graduated from the Westward Ho! boarding school (could we make this up?) and returned to the India he had loved as a child, to work as a journalist. For seven years he reported on that exotic land, tapping out some poems on the side. He hit pay dirt at once: *Departmental Ditties* (1886) and *Plain Tales from the Hills* (1888) brought him fame in less than a year. Riding on their crest, he returned to England

THE PRE-RAPHAELITES

Pre-Raphaelite painter Dante Gabriel Rossetti (1828–1882).

No, we don't mean television before Ralph and Alice Kramden played cards with Ed and Trixie Norton. The Pre-Raphaelites were a group of English painters, poets, and critics who reacted against Victorian materialism to churn out earnest quasi-religious works inspired by medieval and early Renaissance painters. In 1848, the Pre-Raphaelite Brotherhood was established to revitalize art through a simpler, more positive vision. The big guns in the group included brothers Dante Gabriel and William Michael Rossetti, John Everett Millais, William Holman Hunt, Frederick George Stephens, William Morris, and Edward Burne-Jones (Kipling's uncle).

in 1889. Soon after, he married an American woman, Caroline Balestier. The Kiplings settled in Caroline's family home in Vermont. Over the next four years Kipling wrote some of his best work, which proves the salutary influence of a good woman. As early as 1891, Henry James was calling him a genius; Oscar Wilde slyly modifying that opinion to "a genius who drops his aspirates," an allusion to Kipling's attempt to recreate lower-class dialect.

After the war, taste changed and Kipling began to outlive his reputation. There were some fine children's stories, but Britannia no longer ruled the waves and Kipling no longer ruled the page.

OSCAR WILDE: THE IMPORTANCE OF BEING OSCAR

Oscar Wilde (1854–1900). Irish writer, wit, aesthete, fabulante.

Oscar Wilde (1854–1900), foot soldier in the aesthetic movement, was a charming, flamboyant dandy who delighted in wit and verbal word play. Although he penned some serious works, chief among them his 1891 novel *The Picture of Dorian Gray*, he is primarily remembered today for such droll plays as *The Importance of Being Earnest* (1895), a send-up of Victorian earnestness, and for his homosexual liaison with Lord Alfred Douglas. The latter would likely have run its course had not Wilde recklessly sued Lord Alfred's father, the marquess of Queensberry, for libel. Since Oscar did swing both ways, there was no libel, and he landed in jail for not treading the straight and narrow. The public's reaction against what they saw as perversion was so violent that Wilde was completely ruined. He died three years later.

KIM: A BOY AND HIS LAMA

A daring trendsetter, Kim took to the streets long before it became a fashionable alternate lifestyle in major American cities. Left to his own devices when his parents died, young Kim survives by his wits in Lahore's teeming alleys. A Tibetan lama, searching for the holy river, drops into town. Seeking adventure and a way to advance the

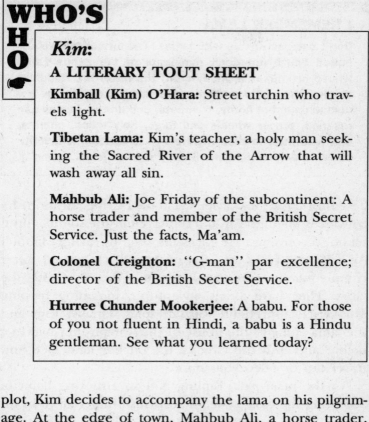

WHO'S WHO

Kim:

A LITERARY TOUT SHEET

Kimball (Kim) O'Hara: Street urchin who travels light.

Tibetan Lama: Kim's teacher, a holy man seeking the Sacred River of the Arrow that will wash away all sin.

Mahbub Ali: Joe Friday of the subcontinent: A horse trader and member of the British Secret Service. Just the facts, Ma'am.

Colonel Creighton: "G-man" par excellence; director of the British Secret Service.

Hurree Chunder Mookerjee: A babu. For those of you not fluent in Hindi, a babu is a Hindu gentleman. See what you learned today?

plot, Kim decides to accompany the lama on his pilgrimage. At the edge of town, Mahbub Ali, a horse trader, gives Kim a secret message to deliver to a British officer at Umballa.

On the road, Kim and the lama chitchat up the riffraff, and decide to join an old lady traveling in the family bullock cart attended by eight men. Who could pass up a chance like this? At dusk, they meet up with the Mavericks, the regiment Kim's father had served in before he died of drugs and drink, who decide to send Kim to

---

I REMEMBER LAMA . . . .
Don't confuse llamas with lamas. The former are woolly-haired South American ruminants of the genus *Lama* whose fur makes a pricey coat; the latter are Buddhist monks who recite prayers three times a day to the accompaniment of horns, trumpets, and drums. Lamas use rosaries, prayer wheels and flags, holy relics, charms, and talismans in their mystical incantations. A favorite chant is *om mani padme h'um* ("O lotus jewel, amen").

---

be educated at St. Xavier's school. During vacation, he convinces Mahbub Ali to let him rejoin the soldiers until school reconvenes. He earns his keep by saving Mahbub Ali's life and picks up a few neat spy tricks as well. After completing his education, Kim hits the road with the lama. They have a few adventures, including helping Mookerjee apprehend Russian spies. Finally, Kim and the lama come to the house of the woman they had met before and find the river of life on her land. See how travel can broaden your mind?

For the most part, Kipling had an annoying habit of accepting the caste system and British imperialism in his works. *Kim* is a notable exception. Like E. M. Forster's classic novel, *A Passage to India, Kim* does not toe the imperialist party line. An affectionate account of the Indian masses, the novel instead provides insights into India's streets and bazaars at the turn of the century, a time when such stuff was highly exotic to readers back home in England. His picture of Indian life is also remarkably free of sentimentality, and includes graphic passages of opium use, extortion, and fighting.

Many critics regard *Kim* as Kipling's masterpiece. Kim is torn between the life of the courageous, resourceful, and bold (represented by his work as a spy) and the life of contemplation (represented by the lama). But Kim's choice has been made for him by the society in which he has been brought up. It is his destiny to be the man of action, not contemplation. "It is too high for me," he says, when the lama has preached his most moving sermon. But his imagination—and ours—has been affected by the knowledge that there is another way to live one's life.

The book is a masterpiece in style as well as theme. Kipling's gift for creating colorful details to evoke a setting is shown in the crowd scenes as well as the carefully-

E. M. FORSTER

E. M. Forster (1879–1970).

Novelist Edward Morgan Forster (1879–1970) was a linchpin in the Bloomsbury Group, a gaggle of writers, artists, and critics who seemed to spend most of their time trying to keep track of who was sleeping with whom. Included among these randy intellectuals were Lytton Strachey, Virginia Woolf, Vanessa Bell, Clive Bell, Roger Fry, and John Maynard Keynes. Forster's best-selling novel is *A Passage to India* (1924), a scathing castigation of British colonialism and a searching exploration of human relationships. Today, film producers Ismail Merchant and James Ivory produce gorgeous screen versions of Forster's novels that make for great dates.

crafted individual portraits. The descriptions are so vivid that readers can almost taste the coriander in the stew (and maybe smell the sacred cows).

YO HO, IT'S A SAILOR'S LIFE FOR ME

Rich, spoiled Harvey Cheyne is bound for England on an ocean liner. He is so busy retching over the side that he is almost grateful when a huge wave washes him overboard. A passing fisherman plucks him from the briny deeps and plunks him on the *We're Here*, a fishing schooner. The boat's owner, Disko Troop, is distinctly underwhelmed by his uninvited guest, especially when the lad tries to throw his weight around and demands to be

WHO'S WHO

Captains Courageous:
A LITERARY TOUT SHEET

Harvey Cheyne: The poor little rich boy who learns to filet a cod with the best of them.

Disko Troop: Captain of the fishing vessel *We're Here*. A man's man.

Dan Troop: Disko's son, mighty handy on a schooner. A man's boy.

Mr. Cheyne: Harvey's father, the Rockefeller of the railroad set.

taken to New York at once. Doubting that Harvey's daddy is really a millionaire, Troop (played by Spencer Tracy in the movie version) punches the scamp in the nose to teach him to respect his elders. The captain's son, Dan, befriends the poor little rich boy. Despite himself, Harvey adjusts to life aboard a fishing vessel and soon learns the ropes.

At the end of the fishing season, the *We're Here* has once again hauled the most cod and halibut, earning it honors in the fleet and a tidy profit. After the fishing season, the boat docks in Gloucester and Harvey wires Daddy that he is alive and well and even reasonably good with a sextant. The crew is astonished to learn that Harvey is really a rich kid. The Cheynes are overjoyed that Harvey is alive, but they are even happier that he's no longer a brat. Disko Troop and the crew refuse to accept a reward, likely figuring that dumping the kid is payment enough. All's well that ends well.

I LOVE IT WHEN YOU'RE A BRUTE

Captains Courageous extols the value of a life of self-reliance and action. Kipling equated America's "Captains Courageous"—pioneers like Daniel Boone, Kit Carson, and the fictional railroad magnate King Cheyne—with such bold Elizabethan adventurers as Sir Francis Drake, Sir John Hawkins, and Sir Walter Raleigh. America's captains of land and sea were blood brothers to England's earlier adventurers, sharing the same bold spirit and success. Kipling, the nearsighted, bookish, fragile butt of jokes, admired manly men who got the trains to run on time. *Captains Courageous* is vintage Kipling in its emphasis on loyalty and respect, submitting to authority, and belonging.

The Jungle Book

The Jungle Book, likely Kipling's most famous work, revolves around the Mowgli stories, which describe the laughing, fearless man-cub brought up by wolves and taught the Law of the Jungle by his friends Baloo, the wise old bear, and Bagheera, the black panther. Mowgli's sworn enemy, the tiger Shere Khan, lurks in the nearby woods. Other stories in the volume include *Rikki-Tikki-Tavi*, about a plucky little mongoose who takes on two deadly cobras; and *Toomai of the Elephants*, which describes the dance of the elephants. Generations of chil-

*Mowgli and friend in the 1942 film version
of* The Jungle Book.

WHO'S WHO

The Jungle Book:
A LITERARY TOUT SHEET

Mowgli: An Indian boy who lives with the wolves.

Father and Mother Wolf: Mowgli's animal "parents."

Shere Khan: The villainous tiger condemned to wear stripes for killing a man.

Akela: The leader of the wolves.

Bagneera: The black panther.

Baloo: The bear who, along with the panther Bagneera, teaches Mowgli the law of the jungle.

Kaa: The python.

Hathi: The elephant.

Messua: Indian woman who believes that Mowgli is her lost son.

dren have read these stories with great delight, but they're not for kids only.

All the stories in *The Jungle Book* are fables. Kipling believed that moral law is codified by custom and its recognition and preservation is the touchstone of civilization. Those who ignore "the Law" become, in Kipling's unfortunate phrase, "lesser breeds." It is the measure of

Kipling's artistry that the fable beckons us to a place where we must think for ourselves about the issues that underlie these beguiling tales.

The Man Who Would Be King

Written in 1888, when Kipling was twenty-two years old, *The Man Who Would be King* takes off from an incident in Kipling's own life: the narrator, a journalist on assignment, enters into a conversation with Peachy Carnehan, a low-class English adventurer, and promises to give a message to Daniel Dravot, Peachy's partner. The narrator passes along the message when he arrives at Marwar Junction. Soon after, Peachy and Daniel appear and tell the narrator about their plan to rule Kafiristan, an almost unknown territory in what we presume to be the Himalayas (though the film based on the book was actually shot in Morocco's Atlas mountains, and the

WHO'S WHO

The Man Who Would Be King:
A LITERARY TOUT SHEET

The narrator: A reporter, often identified with Kipling himself.

Peachy Carnehan: Soldier of fortune determined to be a king.

Daniel Dravot: The red-bearded dominant partner who also aspires to a throne.

high-altitude Asian natives were thus played by North African Berber tribesmen).

The narrator barely takes the two seriously, but soon finds that they are both resourceful and intelligent. After seeing the movie, we know better: how can you go wrong with Michael Caine and Sean Connery? Peachy and Daniel load the camels, set off, and eventually make it to the throne.

Three years later, the reporter looks up to find a ragged bundle of a man standing by his desk. It's Peachy Carnehan, who recounts the savage end of the story. Daniel has died a horrifying death and Peachy is barely sane, but for one glorious moment they ruled an empire.

AND NOW FOR SOMETHING COMPLETELY DIFFERENT . . . KIPLING'S POETRY

Written at a time when the great English poets were turning inward toward allusion and inference, Kipling's poetry remains a very public art. As a result, his verse suffers from the problem of being perhaps *too* accessible. Some ultrasophisticated modern poetry seemingly can't be appreciated by anyone who doesn't know a few dead languages; whereas just about anyone who's not dead can understand Kipling. Furthermore, Kipling uses rhymes, and we all know that rhymes are o-u-t—except on syrupy greeting cards with embossed flowers.

For poetic inspiration, Kipling drew from the popular culture of nineteenth-century England, from both ends of the scale: songs of the music hall and of the church.

He learned popular tunes and hung around the bar-rooms and barrack halls. Research has its rewards.

Kipling's best-known poems are found in a collection called *Barrack-Room Ballads*, dedicated to "Tommy Atkins," a name he created to stand for the ordinary British soldier. The ballads include *Danny Deever*, *Tommy*, and *Gunga Din*, Kipling's tribute to the Indian water carriers,

---

GUNGA DIN

The famous refrain goes:
He was "Din! Din! Din!
You limping lump o' brick-dust, Gunga Din!
Hi! *slippy hitherao!*
Water, get it! *Panee lao!*
You Squidgy-nosed old idol, Gunga Din!"

*"I'm going to scout around a little.
You take the 600 into the Valley of Death."*

most often recited on a Friday night when some junior VP has had one too many.

Recessional

As poet laureate of England, Kipling was called upon at all major state occasions to scribble down some suitably jingoistic poem. The 1897 Diamond Jubilee to honor the sixtieth anniversary of Queen Victoria's reign was no exception. The occasion prompted a great deal of chest-thumping and boasting about the strength and greatness of the empire. Kipling responded to the celebration by writing *Recessional*, and as far as Her Majesty was concerned, he blew it, though history has been far kinder. Rather than wave the banner for Queen and country, Kipling seized the opportunity to remind the people of England that the British Empire might not last forever.

In both form and title, the poem gets a good right jab

THE SUN NEVER SETS ON THE BRITISH EMPIRE

During the Victorian age, Britannia ruled the waves and the land. Great Britain's smashing victory in the Napoleonic Wars at the beginning of the century had left her the undisputed naval power—which gave the island-nation control over most of the world's commerce. Furthermore, England was the world's leader in manufacturing. Military and economic power helped Britain acquire new colonies around the globe. Victorians could (and did) boast that "the sun never set on the British Empire."

at the underbelly of the empire. A recessional is a hymn sung at the end of a religious service. Ironically, the poem serves to herald the end of the empire rather than assure its long life, for leaks had already sprung in the imperial dike. There was that nasty 1857 mutiny against the British in India; the Boer War would erupt in South Africa in 1899. Nationalism was rearing its ugly head in Australia, and World War I would not be kind. Kipling predicted this collapse in his disparaging references to the bonfires lighted around the world to celebrate the Queen's anniversary. The refrain—"Lest we forget, lest we forget!"—heaps on the guilt.

British soldiers in South Africa during the Boer War,
as the sun begins to set on the British Empire.

SUMMARY

 Kipling was one of the great masters of the short story. Some critics claim that he is the greatest short-story writer England has ever produced.

 As standard-bearer for British imperialism, he has come under fire, but there's nothing wrong with a little patriotism. OK, a lot.

 He was a superb craftsman; the swinging Benny Goodman of poetic rhythms.

CHAPTER 9

ROBERT LOUIS STEVENSON
(1850–1894)

YOU MUST REMEMBER THIS

Stevenson created the swashbuckling adventure story without the obligatory moralistic ending and thus provided years of gainful employment to such movie stars as Douglas Fairbanks (Jr. and Sr.) and Errol Flynn. He also established a memorable cast of characters who have become part of our culture: the dual personality Dr. Jekyll and Mr. Hyde, the piratical Long John Silver, and countless talking parrots. And we cannot forget that Stevenson gave us the words to that immortal drinking song: "Fifteen men on the Dead Man's Chest; yo-ho-ho and a bottle of rum!"

MOST FAMOUS FOR

Having as many words in his name as he had famous books:

★ *Treasure Island* (1883)
★ *Kidnapped* (1886)
★ *The Strange Case of Dr. Jekyll and Mr. Hyde* (1886)

REBEL WITH A CAUSE

Robert Louis Balfour Stevenson was born in Edinburgh, Scotland, in 1850. A sickly child, he nonetheless did so well at school that he was able to enter Edinburgh University when he was sixteen.

Stevenson's family expected him to become a lighthouse engineer, the family profession, but Stevenson picked law instead. Having escaped from his family's reach, Stevenson ditched classes, wrote for the university magazine, and lived a bohemian life. When he was twenty-three, our hero developed a severe respiratory infection and went to the French Riviera to regain his strength.

Stevenson's excursion abroad convinced him that the law was no life for a man with a brain and a buck. He passed the bar to please the folks, threw the torts out the window, and took to the road. Soon after, Stevenson fell in love with Fanny Osbourne, a Fallen Woman. Fanny was (1) separated from her husband; (2) ten years older than Stevenson; and (3) worst of all (gasp!) an American!

In 1878, Mrs. Osbourne returned to her home in California to try to obtain a divorce, and Stevenson decided to follow his beloved. In 1880, Fanny was granted her

BOHEMIANS: LIFE IN THE FAST LANE
Bohemians were artists and writers who disregarded the conventions of polite society. They scandalized the local yokels with their sexual license, really bad clothes, and rantings about bourgeois hypocrisy.

divorce and quickly married her young, unemployed, and sickly suitor. The newlyweds honeymooned at an abandoned silver mine, perhaps hoping to strike it rich. Curiously, they did: the marriage proved remarkably happy and soon after, Stevenson *père* relented and offered the couple his financial backing.

The warmth of his family's welcome persuaded Stevenson and his bride to stay in Scotland, and they rented a cottage in the Highlands. Here Stevenson wrote *Treasure*

TUBERCULOSIS: THE WHITE PLAGUE

Stevenson suffered from tuberculosis, a disease of the lungs. For centuries, tuberculosis was one of the most feared of all diseases—during the nineteenth century, TB and its complications claimed one in five lives. The disease was a cruel critic, snuffing out many a literary light: Charlotte, Emily, Anne, and Branwell Brontë; John Keats; and Katherine Mansfield; to mention just a few. Since no one had any idea what caused or cured TB, the standard treatment was a sojourn in the country, which served to isolate the highly-contagious patient and, remarkably, often effect a (temporary) recovery.

The look of those wasting away from the disease helped to create the prevailing nineteenth-century standard of female beauty: bright eyes, translucent skin, and red lips. Despite all their efforts, doctors remained powerless against the "white plague" until 1882, when self-trained German bacteriologist Robert Koch identified the rodlike bacillus. The final step came in 1944 with the discovery of streptomycin by Ukrainian-born Selman Waksman. Tragically, the disease is reasserting itself once again today, especially in urban centers.

Island. Published in 1883, the book was an instant hit, igniting his literary career. Encouraged by its success, Stevenson wrote another adventure story, *The Black Arrow* and, in 1886, what many consider his best work, *Kidnapped*. But the adulation was not enough to stave off a fierce lung hemorrhage and the Stevensons took refuge in England. He continued to write and, in 1886, produced *The Strange Case of Dr. Jekyll and Mr. Hyde*, the masterpiece about a physician with a split personality, a book that inspired countless Creature Features and Classic Comics.

In 1887, the Stevensons finally got decent travel advice and sailed for America. Our hero stepped off the boat

"I read 'The Day Dr. Jekyll Was Kidnapped From Treasure Island.' *Interesting manuscript, Mr. Stevenson, but I rather think you have enough here for three novels, old chap."*

in New York in 1887 to find himself a full-fledged literary lion. The family basked in the glow of his celebrity, hit the hot spots, and finally, in 1888, settled down for the winter in the Adirondacks, where they hoped the mountain air would do him some good. But the winter was bitter rather than salutary and Stevenson eagerly accepted his publisher's offer to write a book about the South Seas. Can we talk? Would anybody turn down an offer like this?

Stevenson chartered a yacht (publishers' advances must have been pretty sweet in those days) and set sail for the South Seas. After visiting Father Damien's leper colony on the Hawaiian island of Molokai, the family dropped anchor in Samoa. He built a house on the top of a mountain and settled in. But this paradise was fleeting: he died the same year. Ironically, the cause of death was a brain hemorrhage, not the tuberculosis that had plagued him all his life.

TREASURE ISLAND:
X MARKS THE SPOT

Treasure Island traces the adventures of young Jim Hawkins, who sets off with Dr. Livesey and Squire Trelawney to find buried treasure. They are nearly thwarted by the crew of their ship, the *Hispaniola,* especially the clever one-legged pirate Long John Silver, but good prevails and they eventually find the treasure with the help of Ben Gunn, a castaway sailor on Treasure Island. Here are the details:

Jim's father managed the Admiral Benbow Inn on the English seacoast. One day a drunken sailor comes to stay

WHO'S
H
O ☞

Treasure Island:
A LITERARY TOUT SHEET

Jim Hawkins: The teenage hero and narrator of the story; the stuff a girl's dreams are made of.

Old Blind Pew: The fearsome blind pirate who comes tapping into the Admiral Benbow Inn, in search of a treasure map.

Long John Silver: The cook on the *Hispaniola*, nicknamed "Barbecue," who subsequently lent his name to countless fast-food fish joints and porn stars. Shiver me timbers.

Dr. Livesey: The good doctor who isn't afraid of man nor beast.

Squire Trelawney: On the side of the good guys; helps set up the *Hispaniola*, its crew, and the voyage.

Ben Gunn: Our Man Friday: the castaway who proves that out of sight isn't out of mind.

Captail Smollett: Captain courageous of the *Hispaniola*.

Cap'n Flint: Silver's parrot. Most memorable (and only) line: "Pieces of eight!"

Buccaneers: Party crashers of the worst sort; they never bring their own bottle of rum.

and terrify the locals. After he dies, Jim and his mother discover a treasure map in his sea chest. Dr. Livesey, Squire Trelawney, and Jim decide to boldly go where no man has gone before and find the treasure.

Jim meets Long John Silver and is enthralled by the cook's tales of life on the high seas, but we know better—we've seen the movie. Captain Smollett shares his misgivings about the lack of security and the presence of razor-sharp cutlery, especially when all anyone seems to be eating are apples.

Silver plans to mutiny and steal the treasure. On the island, Jim gives Silver the slip and finds Ben Gunn, marooned on the island for three years. The mutineers attack; the battle is bloody but not decisive. Ben Gunn finds the treasure and the survivors load it onto the *Hispaniola* and set sail. No trust fund in sight: they are set upon by marauders and Silver escapes in the confusion with a sack of coins. Jim is haunted by the parrot's ghostly cry, "Pieces of eight! Pieces of eight!"

Treasure Island is one of the most satisfying adventure stories ever told, because it is one of the most unhampered. Stevenson jettisons geographical place and time and the demands that go with them. Jim Hawkins refuses to reveal the location of the island, because "there is treasure not yet lifted"; he explains he is going to relate the history of "the year 17—," but like other historical romanticists, fails to fill in the last two digits. Personality is dispensed with as well, for all but one of the pirates (Long John Silver) are interchangeable figures who don or doff disguises at will. Death becomes equally casual. Although people drop on all sides, Stevenson is cavalier about mortality, as befits an adventure story. All this

---

CAREER CORNER: BE A PIRATE!

Pleasure your name, adventure your game? Looking for loot in all the wrong places? Then a pirate's life is for you! You'll follow in the noble steps of the English, French, and Dutch sea adventurers who preyed on the Caribbean and the Pacific seaboard of South America in the second half of the seventeenth century. Stevenson wasn't the only one to craft fiction from the facts of such adventurous lives; Jonathan Swift and Daniel Defoe were also influenced by these brave, cruel macho men. Buccaneers were largely inspired by the example of such sixteenth-century seamen as Sir Francis Drake, but unlike Drake, their commissions were rarely valid. By the end of the seventeenth-century, however, the life of plunder and pleasure had come to a close, when these freebooters became legitimate privateers in the service of their respective nations.

---

was deliberate. In *A Gossip on Romance,* Stevenson wrote: "There is a vast deal in life and letters . . . where the interest turns on the problems of the body and of the practical intelligence, in clean open-air adventure, the shock of arms or the diplomacy of life."

DR. JEKYLL AND MR. HYDE:
HYDE AND SEEK

Stevenson first dreamed up the plot of Dr. Jekyll and Mr. Hyde in a nightmare—proof that you should watch what you eat before you go to sleep. He jotted down the outline and read it to his wife. She so vehemently objected to the Poe-like character of Hyde that Stevenson threw the first draft in the fire. Haunted by the plot (or too many pepperonis, maybe) he began the story again. This time it pleased Fanny, and the rest is literary and cinematic history.

Dr. Henry Jekyll, a kindly physician, becomes fascinated with the idea that at least two different entities—

WHO'S WHO

Dr. Jekyll and Mr. Hyde: A LITERARY TOUT SHEET

Dr. Henry (Harry) Jekyll: The good guy. This middle-aged wunderkind concocts a strange potion that unleashes the evil side of his personality. The experiment gets out of hand when the evil "twin" within him, who takes the name Edward Hyde, refuses to hide again.

Edward Hyde: The bad guy. An in-your-face kind of lunatic given to sexual perversion and other wild and crazy hobbies.

Gabriel John Utterson: A lawyer who nonetheless represents a highly moral and upright person—you know, the kind of pal who would never let you cheat off his paper in algebra.

Dr. Hastie Lanyon: Meek and mild Dr. Milquetoast; the traditional scientist so unnerved by the revelation of the evil within us all that he dies of shock.

EDGAR ALLAN POE

Edgar Allan Poe (1809–1849).

Edgar Allan Poe (1809–1849) is known for his debauchery, alcoholism, and marriage to his fourteen-year-old cousin, Virginia. In his spare time, he created the detective story, defined the modern short story, and wrote some trenchant literary criticism. Makes you wonder what he would have accomplished sober.

and perhaps more—occupy a person's body. Can he separate these entities? Of course he can, Gentle Reader, or we wouldn't have a novel. So the good doctor invents an evil brew that transforms him into a repulsive creature, Edward Hyde, who represents the "pure evil" that exists within. Now Jekyll can commit acts of evil and feel no guilt; furthermore, he can drink the same potion and be transformed back into his original self.

As a symbol not noted for its subtlety, Hyde represents the sexual aspect of men (Victorian women didn't have sex, silly) that Stevenson's contemporaries felt the need to hide, much as they covered the legs of tables as well as other, more supple (not to mention living) limbs. Hyde comes to represent pure evil for evil's sake. He is much smaller and younger than Jekyll, suggesting that we have more good than evil in us and that evil develops earlier in life than good (or maybe that evil just ages better).

Everything proceeds merrily, until Hyde murders Sir

DR. JEKYL and MR. ED

Danvers Carew. Repelled by his action, Jekyll pals around with his old buddies for a while to shake off his mad-slasher alter ego. But Hyde won't hide, and one sunny day Jekyll is transformed into Hyde smack in the middle of Regent's Park. The evil part of Jekyll's character begins to prevail; the original potion will no longer effect the transformation. Jekyll is trapped as Hyde!

Jekyll realizes that the original compound must have been imbued with an impurity he cannot duplicate. In despair, he commits suicide to rid himself of Hyde, but since suicide is forbidden by religious law, Jekyll's act allows Hyde to become dominant. The dying Jekyll becomes Hyde in the final death throes. Can't keep a good villain down, we always say.

When *Dr. Jekyll and Mr. Hyde* was published, some people criticized Stevenson for using drugs to effect the personality change. Henry James called it "too explicit and explanatory"; but to our own generation, which takes the change or control of personality by drugs for granted, Jekyll's potion does not seem especially unrealistic. For us, the true novelty of the story is in the physical transformation of Dr. Jekyll into Mr. Hyde, and it is this that gives the book its universal appeal. It was the idea of the total incarnation of a good man's evil nature

DOUBLE YOUR PLEASURE, DOUBLE YOUR FUN

Fyodor Dostoyevsky (1821–1881), Russian novelist who toyed with the idea of the doppelgänger.

Stevenson is playing off the legend of the doppelgänger, a very popular notion at the end of the nineteenth century. According to this legend, everyone has a second, darker self, called a doppelgänger. This twin is usually invisible, but may become visible at certain times. In Dostoyevsky's *The Double,* for example, a poor clerk sees his own double, who has succeeded where the clerk has failed. Conrad's *The Secret Sharer* (see chapter on Conrad) is built around a doppelgänger. One dark night, a young sea captain rescues a murderer—his double—from the ocean. The captain hides his double and has visions of his own darker side. The narrator of Poe's *William Wilson* is hounded by his double, who speaks only in a whisper. (And you thought this kind of stuff only happened after that third bottle of tequila.)

into a monster, which fascinated Victorian readers and holds our interest today.

In 1894, a critic wrote that the book "stands behind *Pilgrim's Progress* and *Gulliver's Travels* as one of the three great allegories in English." In fact, the story had no serious implications at all until Mrs. Stevenson made her

*The popularity of Stevenson's classic
has endured into the twentieth century.*

TAKE THE MONEY AND RUN

Fame is fickle and, as with most writers, Stevenson's reputation has fluctuated. Much celebrated after the publication of *Dr. Jekyll and Mr. Hyde,* Stevenson's standing went into eclipse soon after his death, and he was considered little more than a mannered essayist. But by the 1950s the pendulum had swung back, and he once again was seen as a writer of great originality and power, celebrated for his brilliant adventure stories.

husband rewrite it and add a "moral dimension." In the novel, Stevenson probes the Calvinist tradition of personified evil. By looking deeply into the soul of a seemingly good man, Stevenson reveals the possibility of evil within even the most upright people.

KIDNAPPED: WHAT DO THEY WEAR UNDER THOSE KILTS?

It's 1751. Stevenson's hero, David Balfour, a Scottish boy of seventeen, sets off from his family home following the death of his father and mother to seek his rightful inheritance as Lord of the House of Shaws. Through an agreement made between his father and uncle, David was to receive his title upon the death of his father, but his treacherous uncle arranges to have David kidnapped by the evil Captain Hoseason of the *Covenant*, a trading brig, and sold into slavery in the Carolinas, a little corner of the then-new colonies. Through a chance collision at sea with a small boat, David meets the Jacobite rebel, Alan Breck.

Although politically on opposite sides of the fence (Balfour is loyal to the King and Breck is a Jacobite) the two lose the attitude and become friends after the *Covenant* is wrecked off the coast of Mull. They narrowly escape being arrested for a murder they witness. The dangerous journey across the Highlands makes up most of the plot, and the novel ends as Breck secures Balfour's inheritance for him and the friends part. In a nutshell, it's the story of a young man's odyssey to maturity and self-reliance. Despite the dialect, it's a good read.

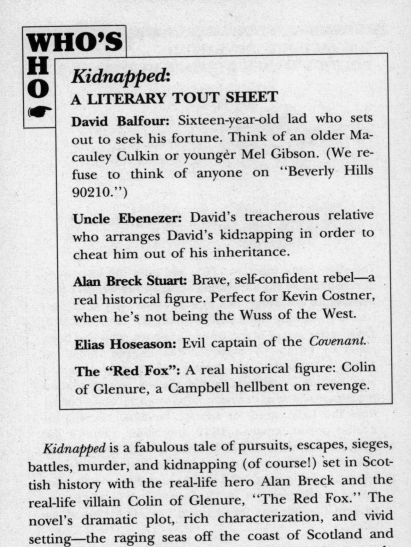

**WHO'S
H O** ☞

Kidnapped:
A LITERARY TOUT SHEET

David Balfour: Sixteen-year-old lad who sets out to seek his fortune. Think of an older Macauley Culkin or youngèr Mel Gibson. (We refuse to think of anyone on "Beverly Hills 90210.")

Uncle Ebenezer: David's treacherous relative who arranges David's kidnapping in order to cheat him out of his inheritance.

Alan Breck Stuart: Brave, self-confident rebel—a real historical figure. Perfect for Kevin Costner, when he's not being the Wuss of the West.

Elias Hoseason: Evil captain of the *Covenant.*

The "Red Fox": A real historical figure: Colin of Glenure, a Campbell hellbent on revenge.

Kidnapped is a fabulous tale of pursuits, escapes, sieges, battles, murder, and kidnapping (of course!) set in Scottish history with the real-life hero Alan Breck and the real-life villain Colin of Glenure, "The Red Fox." The novel's dramatic plot, rich characterization, and vivid setting—the raging seas off the coast of Scotland and the country's hauntingly wild countryside—have made the book popular with young readers for decades. Yet

THE JACOBITE MOVEMENT: POLITICS MAKES STRANGE BEDFELLOWS

James I of England (1566–1625). His mom lost her head, but he nevertheless managed to bring the Stuart line to the British throne.

The story takes place in 1751, just after the last series of rebellions by the Jacobites, Scottish Highlanders who believed in the Stuart line of succession to the English throne. Following the death of Queen Elizabeth in 1603, James (the son of Mary, Queen of Scots, who had been killed by Elizabeth) ascended the English throne as James I of England and James VI of Scotland. James was a Stuart, and thus by his actions he established the Stuart line of succession. (The word Jacobite comes from the Latin word for James, *Jacobus*.) Except for a brief period between 1649 and 1660, James's descendants ruled until 1714, when George Louis of Hanover got the head seat at the table. The Jacobites, a few thousand strong, tried unsuccessfully to regain control of the throne, first in 1715 and again in 1745. Our modern Charles and Diana could use such support as this.

Alexandre Dumas (1802–1870). Author of The Three Musketeers *and* The Count of Monte Cristo, *a major influence on Stevenson's novels.*

the book retains its lure for adult readers as well.

Writing in 1887, no less an august literary critic than Henry James called *Kidnapped* Stevenson's best novel to date, saying it was superior to the work of Stevenson's own favorite author, Alexandre Dumas. In *Kidnapped,* Stevenson fused his deep feelings for Scotland's history, character, and atmosphere with his research into eighteenth-century Scottish history to create a kind of thrilling docudrama, a skillful blend of actual and fictitious events.

SUMMARY

⏱ Stevenson made it possible for us to round up the usual suspects: the split-personality Jekyll/Hyde, the swashbuckling Long John Silver, the squawking parrot.

⏱ He wrote pure adventure stories without the obligatory moralistic ending, creating dashing heroes who populate many a B-movie.

⏱ A master of horror and suspense, he used mood and atmosphere to create the magic of a story well told.

CHAPTER 10

THOMAS HARDY

(1840–1928)

YOU MUST REMEMBER THIS

Thomas Hardy obsessed over the conflict between convention and rebellion. Like figures in a ballad or romance, his characters are embodiments of a single ruling passion. Each of his novels traces the arbitrary effect of blind chance upon human destiny.

MOST FAMOUS FOR

His fiction, although his poetry is also highly regarded. Here is a list of his top five novels and a handful of his verse:

- ★ *Far From the Madding Crowd* (1874)
- ★ *The Return of the Native* (1878)
- ★ *The Mayor of Casterbridge* (1886)
- ★ *Tess of the D'Urbervilles* (1891)
- ★ *Jude the Obscure* (1895)
- ★ *Hap, The Darkling Thrush,* and *Ah, Are You Digging on My Grave?*

171

TOM THE OBSCURE

The oldest child of an architect and his pretentious wife, Hardy was born near Dorchester, the town called "Casterbridge" in his literary remapping of southern England. As a child, Hardy learned to walk the walk and talk the talk; that is, he played on the heath and spoke the local dialect. *Home, Sweet Home* would have a powerful effect on his imagination: he would later set most of his novels in an imaginary region modeled on Dorset. The settings were so vivid and so carefully built upon reality that readers with a good sense of direction but a poor grasp of literary license would attempt to follow with maps the travels of his characters, and visit the places in which they lived.

A sickly child, Hardy missed so much school that his parents decided to educate him at home (which isn't a bad threat to one's own child if he attempts to feign a cold). When he was eight years old, Hardy was strong enough to enter the village school. Hardy's father was a builder, and so when the malleable momma's boy turned sixteen he was apprenticed to an architect in Dorchester. More interested in Greek and Latin than in floor plans, he spent his mornings cramming the classics with the schoolmaster next door to the office. In 1862, having served his time with the blueprints, he dutifully went to London to hang out a shingle.

Away from the influence of the 'rents, Hardy spent his time taking night classes at King's College, attending concerts, visiting art museums, and writing poetry and stories. When his poems did not sell, he decided prose was the way to go. His architectural training actually came in handy, for it provided him with the topic for his first published work, a story called *How I Built Myself a House.* He cut his teeth on three apprentice novels. Then in 1874, he struck literary pay dirt with *Far From the Madding Crowd.*

Now firmly wedded to a life of literature, he also took a moment to marry Emma Gifford, a high-spirited church organist, but Hardy proved far more devoted to his writing than to his wife. Neither Hardy's mother nor Emma's was shy about speaking her mind. The mothers-in-law from hell drove a wedge between the couple; Hardy's solitary nature and pessimism finished the job. Soon Hardy was spending several months a year in London, wining and dining sweet young things while Emma tended hearth and home. Two years after her death in 1912, Hardy married Florence Emily Dugdale, who did double duty as secretary.

THE INDUSTRIAL REVOLUTION

Hardy lived in an age of transition, which added a nervous edge to the natural melancholy that pervades his novels. As the Industrial Revolution destroyed agricultural life and shifted population to the cities, Hardy witnessed the disintegration of rural customs which to him had represented security, stability, and dignity for everyone. In this period, many basic social, religious, scientific, and political beliefs were shaken to their roots. Hardy called himself a "meliorist" (one who believes the world can be improved) but don't take his word for it. His rhetorical glass wasn't half empty; it was bone-dry.

Like Dickens and other popular authors of the day, Hardy published all his novels in installments in family magazines before issuing them as books. This method of publication enabled him to reap a tidy sum, but it also laid him open to the strict morals of Victorian England. In *Tess* and *Jude the Obscure,* Hardy rebelled and openly attacked the hypocrisy of his age, in which people didn't always practice the virtues they preached. The backlash against *Jude* was so vicious that Hardy vowed never to publish another novel. For the last thirty years of his life, Hardy licked his wounds and retreated into poetry. The

Hardy strolls with actress Gwen Frangçon-Davies, who played Tess in the stage version of Tess of the D'Urbervilles; *Mrs. Hardy and stage manager Philip Ridgeway follow a few steps behind.*

body of "the last of the Great Victorians" was buried in Westminster Abbey; they left his heart, literally, in Dorset, which he fictionalized as Wessex.

BEST-KNOWN NOVEL

THE RETURN OF THE NATIVE: GOING NATIVE

It's the old theme of a man in love with two women, and a woman in love with two men. Unless you happen to have an exam tomorrow, don't worry overmuch about the names: all of Hardy's characters love the wrong people and no one can pronounce the names anyway.

Sultry Eustacia Vye yearns to marry a man worthy of her and escape Egdon Heath for more exotic lands. She has only one possible candidate: Damon Wildeve, keeper of the village inn. Wildeve, however, sets his sights on sweet Thomasin Yeobright. But through a typically Hardy

---

CAREER NIGHT: YOU'RE GOING TO BE A WHAT?

Diggory Venn is a reddleman. Not a career listed in the Occupational Handbook, you say? "Reddle" describes the red ocher dye used, as cowboys use branding irons, to mark sheep and other creatures too slow to get out of the way. So Diggory spends his days tattooing sheep. Today they actually use soluble spray paint. Who said life on the heath doesn't offer opportunities for artistic expression?

WHO'S WHO ☛

The Return of the Native:
A LITERARY TOUT SHEET

Eustacia Vye: Smoldering country Delilah who represents life sacrificed to convention. Too hot to handle.

Clym Yeobright: Noble hero idealistically returning to his home to teach the rustics.

Damon Wildeve: Lady-killer relegated to life as an innkeeper.

Diggory Venn: Thomasin's self-appointed guardian angel. He's a hunk, even though he's completely red because of the dye he uses in his job as a reddleman.

Thomasin Yeobright: The sweet young thing you love to hate.

Mrs. Yeobright: Quick-tempered, self-pitying mother-in-law who knows a hussy when she sees one.

Captain Vye: Eustacia's grandfather, a former naval officer one sandwich shy of a picnic.

Egdon Heath: The arena of the action, functions as an image, a setting, and even as a character in the novel. The heath personifies the indifference of nature and the hostility of Fate to people's hopes for happiness.

twist of fate, the Wildeve-Yeobright wedding license proves invalid and the marriage cannot proceed.

The arrival of Clym Yeobright stirs Eustacia's ambitions. Clym has left his job as a diamond merchant in Paris to return to the simple life of his youth. He's determined to become a teacher in his native village. Get the title? Eustacia ditches Damon and schemes to marry Yeobright because she thinks he will take her away from all this. To spite Eustacia, Damon marries Thomasin. Against his mother's wishes, Clym marries Eustacia. Clym's determination to stay on the heath thwarts Eustacia's plans to leave it. He studies so hard that he ruins his eyesight (let this be a lesson to you), and finds solace in cutting bushes on the heath.

THE HEATH

About a third of England is heath, rolling hills of peat moss, heather, grass, and bilberry. Like sushi, heath is an acquired taste. The splashes of deep purple bell heather are lovely, but the heath as a whole is a wild, lonely, isolated place.

A stretch of heath—you almost expect to see Gene Kelly and Cyd Charisse tripping through the heather, don't you?

Learning of her Clym's misfortune, his mother relents and calls on the couple. Through a mistake, no one answers the door and she wanders for hours on the heath in the broiling sun. And dies. Clym initially blames himself but later drives Eustacia from the house. She meets Wildeve, ripe with inheritance, and he agrees to help her escape to the seaport, secretly planning to come along for the ride. Everyone meets at the whirlpool just in time to hear Eustacia plop into the raging waters. Wildeve and Clym jump in after her and Wildeve also drowns. In the tacked-on happy ending, Thomasin marries her secret suitor Diggory and Clym becomes a traveling preacher. Have we lost you yet?

CHICKEN LITTLE, THE SKY IS FALLING

Hardy veers between fatalism and determinism: Is life controlled by a great impersonal force independent of human will, or does cause and effect still hold? In the world of his novels, people are like flies in molasses: they have no control over their own lives, struggle as they may. Life's pleasures are fleeting and time can turn joy to ashes. A character's goodness may contain the seed of his or her own downfall. In a character's passionate obsession, we see the power of nature, love, fate, and chance.

Many Victorian authors used chance and coincidence as a means of furthering the plot, but in Hardy such factors become more than mere devices. Fateful incidents, overheard conversations, and missed doorbells symbolize the forces working against characters in their efforts to control their own destiny. The people most in harmony with their environment are usually the most contented, but nature can take on sinister qualities that overcome even the most promising aspirations.

Hardy classified his fiction as *Novels of Character and Environment; Romances and Fantasies;* and *Novels of Ingenuity and Experiment*. He placed *Return of the Native* in the first category. One critic called it a "Tragedy of Cross-Purpose." The novel can also be regarded as the struggle for the soul of a man who is not strong enough to shape his destiny or prevent his women from misshaping it. Or just the story of a really bad hair day.

FOUR OTHER NOVELS BRIEFLY DISCUSSED

TESS OF THE D'URBERVILLES: YOU PLAY, YOU PAY

Discovering that they are descended from an aristocratic family, the Durbeyfields send their eldest daughter, sixteen-year-old Tess, to the neighboring d'Urbervilles to claim kinship. They are, in fact, not related, but that doesn't stop the young heir, Alec d'Urberville, from having his way with our sweet young thing. Pregnant, Tess returns home and has the child, who dies shortly after birth. A year later she goes to a distant farm to work as a dairymaid. There she meets Angel Clare, and they fall in love. Because of her past she feels unwor-

WHO'S WHO ☞

Tess of the D'Urbervilles:
A LITERARY TOUT SHEET

Tess Durbeyfield: Like a virgin: "A Pure Woman Faithfully Presented," as the subtitle asserts. Proud, loyal, and honest, this classy sixteen-year-old deserved better.

Angel Clare: Slave to convention: Hardy's mouthpiece for the controversial subjects of his day.

Alec d'Urberville: The rakish mustached aristocrat, Snidely Whiplash with a heart.

John and Joan Durbeyfield: Tess's parents, the Ma and Pa Kettle of the country village of Marlott. John nurtures his natural aversion to work after he learns that he is descended from nobility.

thy of Clare's love and tries unsuccessfully to confess her sordid past. Only on her wedding night can she get her husband to listen to the story of her seduction. Clare denounces his bride and leaves her to go to Brazil.

To support her family, Tess works as a farm laborer. She meets Alec, who has given up the flesh for the cloth. (Liar, liar, pants on fire.) His religious fervor is soon replaced by sexual ardor and he pursues Tess once again. Tess writes to Angel, imploring him to come home and help her. When she can no longer find work, she consents to live with Alec.

Tess's father dies and the family is turned out of their home. Angel returns from Brazil, repenting of his cruel rejection of his wife. But when Angel finds Tess with Alec, he turns from her again. Tess kills Alec and rushes to catch up with Angel, who forgives her for her misdeed. They spend a few blissful days in a deserted mansion, but Tess's happiness is brief. The police arrest her and she is hanged for murder.

TESS OF THE TURMOIL

The subtitle—*A Pure Woman*—outraged the righteous more than anything else Hardy had ever done. How could a woman seduced at the end of the novel's first phase still have several hundred pages to live? Fortunately, the reading public, which had ignored Hardy's first twelve novels, gave this one a look-see. *Tess* became Hardy's first bestseller.

The novel challenges a rigidly held religious belief that prevailed in England in Hardy's day: The stain of sin can never be erased. By taking the sentimental plot and soaking it in irony, Hardy turns hackneyed convention on its ears.

The dialogue is stilted but there's a great sense of the dramatic—Hardy is the Cecil B. DeMille of the heath. Readers handicapped by a logical mind might be bothered by problems of chance and coincidence in Hardy's novels. But his power lies in his ability to make the implausible seem inevitable.

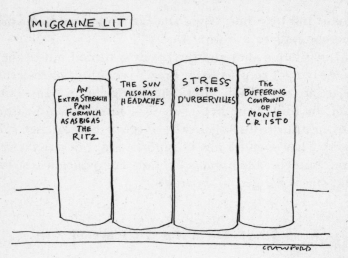

MIGRAINE LIT

AN EXTRA STRENGTH PAIN FORMULA AS AS BIG AS THE RITZ

THE SUN ALSO HAS HEADACHES

STRESS OF THE D'URBERVILLES

The BUFFERING COMPOUND OF MONTE CRISTO

FAR FROM THE MADDING CROWD: TWO'S COMPANY, THREE'S A CROWD

Bathsheba Everdene has three suitors: Gabriel Oak, a shepherd; William Boldwood, a farmer; Sergeant Francis Troy, a dashing soldier. We should all have such problems. What's a girl to do? Bathsheba picks Door #3 and, as is true for most of Hardy's women, it's the wrong one. Bathsheba learns that Troy, her main squeeze, really loves one of her servants, Fanny Robin, whom he abandons after she becomes pregnant.

When Fanny dies in childbirth, Bathsheba learns the truth about Troy's philandering. After erecting a beautiful tombstone for Fanny, Troy leaves Bathsheba, and the police report his presumed death by drowning. People accept the circumstantial evidence of his death, but Bathsheba feels that he is alive. This woman knows her man.

Sure enough, Troy bursts into Boldwood's Christmas party a year later just as the host is proposing to Bathsheba. The infuriated Boldwood kills Troy. Boldwood is tried for murder but cops the insanity plea. Bathsheba marries the loyal Gabriel and lives as happily as is possible in a Hardy novel. As with all of Hardy's novels, Fate, not individual choice, decides the lives of the characters. Providence is hostile; people try to change, but cannot.

WHO'S HO ☞

Far From the Madding Crowd: A LITERARY TOUT SHEET

Bathsheba Everdene: The much-courted heroine.

Gabriel Oak: Bathsheba's suitor, a patient shepherd, honest, kind, and loyal. Makes a good husband.

William Boldwood: Bathsheba's suitor, a gentleman farmer.

Francis Troy: Bathsheba's suitor, the love-'em-and-leave-'em Lothario.

Fanny Robin: The servant whom Francis Troy loves. She gets the shortest end of the short stick.

THE ORIGIN OF SPECIES

Charles Darwin (1809–1882).

Darwin published *The Origin of Species* in 1859. Often referred to as "the book that shook the world," the *Origin* sold out on its first day of publication and subsequently went through six editions. His theory of evolution by natural selection argues that species compete for survival. Those members of a species who survive tend to pass along to subsequent generations whatever favorable physical or mental variations they possess. In addition, Darwin introduced the idea that all related organisms are descended from a common ancestor. The book was a thunderclap in an already stormy world, undermining the prevailing belief in the divine descent of humanity.

THE MAYOR OF CASTERBRIDGE

IT'S A DOG-EAT-DOG WORLD

In a fit of drunken pique during a village fair, Michael Henchard sells his wife Susan and his infant daughter Elizabeth-Jane to a sailor, Edward Newson. When Henchard recovers in the morning, he searches for his family, but his efforts prove in vain. He vows to give up alcohol for twenty-one years. Through hard work and sobriety, he prospers in the town of Casterbridge, where he eventually becomes mayor. Eighteen years later, Susan and Elizabeth-Jane appear in Casterbridge. Out of a sense of guilt, Henchard courts Susan and soon remarries her, hoping that one day he will be able to acknowledge his daughter.

At the same time, Henchard hires a young Scotsman, Donald Farfrae, as his business manager. A short while later, Susan dies and Henchard learns that his own daughter had died many years earlier and that Elizabeth-Jane is really the illegitimate daughter of Newson, the sailor.

Henchard had been involved with Lucetta Templeman, a young woman from the island of Jersey. She travels to Casterbridge so she can marry Henchard, but she meets Farfrae and they fall in love. Henchard fires

WHO'S
WHO
(☞

The Mayor of Casterbridge:
A LITERARY TOUT SHEET

Michael Henchard: The baby- and wife-seller who prospers, only to die a broken man.

Susan Henchard: Michael's wife, no rocket scientist, whose fuzziness shifts the focus to Michael.

Edward Newson: The baby- and wife-buyer, a kindly sailor.

Elizabeth-Jane: The goody-two-shoes daughter of Susan and Newson.

Donald Farfrae: The charming young Scotsman who prospers as Henchard sinks.

Lucetta Templeman: A reckless, shallow hussy; Vanna-White-wannabe.

Farfrae, and the Scotsman sets up his own rival business. Farfrae and Lucetta marry. Henchard's fortunes decline while Farfrae's prosper. The Scotsman becomes mayor. Through a combination of bad luck and bad management, Henchard loses his business and is forced to work for Farfrae. His long-past love affair with Lucetta is revealed and the shock kills her. Nearly broken, Henchard takes refuge with Elizabeth-Jane. Her comfort is the sole bright spot in his life. This is destroyed when Newson reappears and Elizabeth-Jane turns against Henchard.

Farfrae marries Elizabeth-Jane. Henchard dies a broken man.

This novel focuses on one of Hardy's favorite themes: Fate's role in the rise and fall of men's fortunes. Though the novel's dour world view might have satisfied the taste of Calvinist readers, the general public seemed to prefer more optimistic themes, such as the romantic poetry of the poet laureate Alfred, Lord Tennyson, and the dramatic themes of Robert Browning. We continue to read Hardy despite a certain measure of gloom because of his captivating plots (as in a soap opera, you keep hoping for a happy ending), and for his rich depictions of characters and settings.

JUDE THE OBSCURE

JUDE THE OBSCENE: A TRAGEDY OF UNFULFILLED AIMS

This is a divorce lawyer's dream: nearly everyone marries at least twice. Jude and his paramour Sue are caught up in the modern spirit, struggle to break free of the old ways, and fail miserably.

Jude Frawley yearns to attend the university, but because he is poor, he becomes a stonemason. Arabella Donn, a nineteenth-century Valley Girl, deceives him into marriage by making him think he has gotten her pregnant. They have a son, Little Father Time, but the marriage soon breaks up and Arabella heads to Australia to "toss a shrimp on the barbie," as the Aussie tourist board might say.

Free of his wife, Jude goes to Christminster, partly because of his educational dreams but also because his cousin Sue Bridehead is there. He falls in love with her, but she gets engaged to Jude's former teacher, Richard Phillotson. Jude leaves Christminister.

He decides to go to Melchester, study theology, and enter the church at a lower level. Sue now marries Phillotson and, to add insult to injury, at the ceremony Jude gives her away. Arabella and Jude have a brief fling and Jude learns that she has remarried in Australia. Sue eventually leaves her husband; he grants her a divorce, and Sue and Jude embark on a nomadic life. Arabella remarries and sends Jude his son, Little Father Time. Jude and Sue have two children of their own and a third on the way. Their poverty is so great that Jude's son hangs the other children and himself after leaving an explanation, "Done because we are too menny."

The child that Sue is carrying is born dead. Sue and Jude bow to convention. As a form of self-punishment, Sue returns to Phillotson. Jude remarries Arabella, who abuses and neglects him. He dies, alone and miserable, not far from the university that denied him admission.

WHO'S WHO

Jude the Obscure:
A LITERARY TOUT SHEET

Jude Frawley: Let this guy into college already. Jude is obscure because he comes from uncertain origins, struggles to realize his dreams, and dies without having made a mark on the world.

Arabella Donn: No Eva Gabor, she nonetheless marries three times, twice to Jude. Passion without intellect.

Sue Bridehead: Intellect without passion. Baby, it's cold inside.

Richard Phillotson: The Respectable Man, good-hearted and honorable. In short, who cares?

Little Father Time: A name like that has "symbol" written all over it. Sure enough, Jude's Gloomy Gus of a son represents Fate, blighted hopes, and failure.

SORE WINNER

If you thought the mood was grim, consider the style. When Phillotson meets his former student, Arabella, he says: "I should hardly recognize in your present portly self the slim school child you were then.'' Makes you wonder if the author had his writing translated into a foreign tongue and then back again just to spite himself. The style didn't bother the moralists, though; they were too busy savaging the book as "steeped in sex." For modern readers accustomed to fornication televised in increasingly graphic ways, the mere fact of misbehavior hardly excites. But in those days, when a glimpse of ankle could give an aging patient a nocturnal remission, *Jude* had a seismic effect. Dubbing it "Jude the Obscene," some ministers even burned the book. Enraged by the outcry, Hardy stopped writing novels completely. He did continue to write poetry, however, and in fact earned a place in the Poets' Corner of Westminster Abbey with an epic poem called "The Dynasts" (1904–1908), a sweeping verse drama about the Napoleonic Wars.

SUMMARY

 According to Hardy, life is a struggle between people and their fate, and Fate usually wins.

 The world is ruled by chance and circumstance.

 Hardy was a master of place and atmosphere and a compelling storyteller.

CHAPTER 11

HENRY JAMES
(1843–1916)

YOU MUST REMEMBER THIS

One of America's major novelists, critics, and short-story writers; admired for his subtle psychological realism.

MOST FAMOUS FOR

Going out to dinner every night during the whirl of one London social season after writing sizable novels that neatly double as anvils, including:

- ★ *The American* (1877)
- ★ *Daisy Miller* (1878)
- ★ *The Portrait of a Lady* (1881)
- ★ *The Bostonians* (1886)
- ★ *The Princess Casamassima* (1886)
- ★ *The Tragic Muse* (1890)
- ★ *The Turn of the Screw* (1898)
- ★ *The Wings of the Dove* (1902)
- ★ *The Ambassadors* (1903)
- ★ *The Golden Bowl* (1904

TRIVIA CORNER

All told, Henry wrote 114 short stories, 22 novels, 12 (bad) plays, 10 books of lit. crit., 7 travel books, 3 volumes of autobiography, and 2 biographies, a list which may recall to some readers the beleaguered order-taking ship's waiter in *A Night at the Opera,* to whom Groucho Marx says, "Either it's foggy in here or make that two more hard-boiled eggs."

O HENRY!

William James (1842–1910), American philosopher and psychologist.

Henry James was born into a glittering family: they were all wealthy, sophisticated, witty, and successful. Since his father was independently wealthy, he's been described as an "eccentric philosopher"—if he was like the rest of us, we'd call him weird. Big brother William, Henry's intellectual rival, became the first famous American psychologist and likely our most important philosopher. In his spare time William taught at Harvard. Sister Alice has been elevated to the status of feminist saint.

Gee, but life was tough in the James household: From home base in New York City's Washington Square, the troupe regularly decamped to Europe's most glamorous watering holes so the children could pick up that essential *je ne sais quoi.* Henry first traveled to the Continent as an infant, returning again when he was twelve. For the next four years, Henry and his siblings were educated in England, Switzerland, and France by a series of tutors and their father. The family took field trips to the finest museums, libraries, theaters, and galleries on the Continent. When Henry was fifteen, the family moved to the tony rich enclave at Newport, Rhode Island, where he and William studied painting with John LaFarge, a well-known artist. The following year the peripatetic family was back in Europe—Switzerland and Germany.

By the time Henry was a teenager he knew that he wanted to be a writer; soon after, he was publishing reviews and stories in the leading American magazines. In 1869, after a brief stint at Harvard Law School, Henry

The James family spent a good deal of time on steamers such as this, drifting from one fabulous place to another.

moved to England, his base of operations for the rest of his life, and began his career as a writer with the single-minded devotion of a koala with a leafy twig. He never married, and even though he spent a lot of time going out to dinner and was quite gregarious, he lived and worked alone. In 1915, Henry took British citizenship to protest America's lack of involvement in World War I. Many anthologizers refuse to accept his defection, and seizing on some obscure rule of eminent domain, categorize him as an American rather than British writer.

Like Gaul or a stale Scooter Pie, Henry's literary career can be divided into three parts:

Part I: Americans in Europe and Europeans in America. When not dealing with the problems of lost luggage on luxury liners, he chewed on international themes.

Part II: Variety is the spice of life. Henry crafts social and political novels, dramas, and short stories. This is where we get the psychotic children, obsessed men, and haunted houses.

Part III: The Major Phase. Henry returns to international themes and criticism, but with an important twist: the style gets more subtle and allusive. The books he wrote during this time have the reputation of being impenetrable. Be patient, enjoy the accretion of details, don't expect Bruce Willis blowing up Kennedy Airport. The Americans Henry creates during this part of his career may misunderstand how to operate the loo, but they have a freedom, innocence, and grace the Europeans lack.

HENRY TO THE RESCUE

When Henry eagerly stepped into America's literary scene in 1870, he found it cluttered with the carnage of fast-moving adventure stories. In the 1850s, James Fenimore Cooper's swashbuckling heroes had hung around with the last of the Mohicans to raise a little heck; Herman Melville had sailed readers to the exotic South Seas and told the story of a very big whale. Jack London, Bret Harte, and the undisputed master of them all, Mark Twain, picked up on the legacy of adventure with tall tales of the wild west. On the other end of the scale, we had Horatio Alger. In the 1870s, he churned out more than 130 dreadful novels extolling the rewards of luck and pluck.

To Henry, it seemed as though the American novel

MARK TWAIN

Samuel Langhorne Clemens (1835–1910) did more than adopt a nom de plume for safe water on the Mississippi; the whiskey-drinking, cigar-smoking man's man was a wild humorist, bitter satirist, and true moralist. His best book, *The Adventures of Huckleberry Finn* (1883) embodies the dream of innocence and perfect freedom and explores the disastrous effects of slavery on victim and victimizer. James detested Twain's use of the colloquial and vernacular, but what one of his characters says applies to Twain as well: "He could curl his tongue around the bulliest words in the language when he had a mind to, and lay them before you without a jint started, anywheres."

*Mark Twain, né
Samuel Langhorne Clemens
(1835–1910),
contemporary of James.*

was in the hands of parochial barbarians. Who would address the problem of our national identity? Henry to the rescue. He turned to the moral and psychological problems of Americans, analyzing his characters against the backdrop of decadent, deceitful Eurotrash.

REALISM IN JAMES'S NOVELS

James had a tremendous effect on the development of the novel, partly because of his use of realism. If you want to be a stickler, he's not like all the other realists. They "hold a mirror up to life" and make an almost scientific recording of what they see, and it's not a pretty picture. Henry's novels, in contrast, are populated with people you would never encounter in life. His world is too narrow, his detractors complain. H. L. Mencken, for example, suggested that Henry needed a good whiff of the Chicago stockyards to get a little life into his novels.

But Henry James cared little for the hoi polloi. He was interested in his own people, those who had the bucks to devote themselves to the finer things in life. His novels are realistic because his characters act consistently, never violating the parameters of their natures as set up in the novel. The core of his work is layered detail, psychological insights, and minute observations that take the place of action. His mastery of the psychological aspect of characterization developed the art of the novel to a new level.

THE ART OF FICTION

The Art of Fiction was James's most famous and influential critical essay. He wrote it in response to a lecture by English novelist Walter Besant in 1884. In the essay he called fiction "a house of many windows," and wrote: "The only reason for the existence of a novel is that it does attempt to represent life . . . the air of reality seems to me to be the supreme virtue of a novel— the merit on which all its other merits . . . helplessly and submissively depend."

PORTRAIT OF A LADY

DAYS OF WHINE AND POSES

Isabel Archer lives in Albany, New York. After her father dies, her aunt comes to take her away from all that to all this: Europe. She is ready to charm and be charmed and quickly stacks up suitors like planes over the Los Angeles airport. First comes her cousin Ralph; her uncle, Mr. Touchett; and the nobleman of the realm, Lord

WHO'S
H
O

Portrait of a Lady:
A LITERARY TOUT SHEET

Isabel Archer: Tender young thing with a brain, and a mission to be all that she can be.

Ralph Touchett: Isabel's protector; he tries to ensure her happiness with a juicy legacy, but he should know that money can't buy love.

Madame Merle: Sounds like a pricey hairstylist but she's really a dicey dilettante who sacrifices substance for form.

Gilbert Osmond: Self-centered, indolent egotist seeking young American girl for domination; inheritance a plus. Photo a must.

Caspar Goodwood: Good and solid like an oak coffee table, with about the same allure.

Pansy Osmond: Daughter of Gilbert and a (yawn) sweet young thing.

Lord Warburton: Member of the English peerage, suitor of Isabel, and a swell guy. And Isabel goes for Osmond instead. Go figure.

Warburton. Naturally, Lord Warburton immediately falls in love with her. She turns down his proposal to maintain her Freedom. Soon after, her friend Henrietta Stackpole arrives in England with the news that Isabel's transcontinental suitor, Caspar Goodwood, is hot to trot. Caspar proposes, but Isabel again heeds the call of the wild. She promises to touch base in two years.

Hearing that her uncle is ill in London, Isabel hurries

THE AMERICAN-EUROPEAN OPEN

OK, they may have the Louvre, Versailles, and the Sistine Chapel, but we have cable, big refrigerators, and Pez. Henry was the first novelist to address the theme of America *versus* Europe. Almost all his novels concern The American Abroad, which allowed him to compare the spontaneous, morally innocent American to the artificial, evil aristocrat. Here's a quick crib sheet:

American		European
innocence	v.	experience
freedom	v.	custom
sincerity	v.	urbanity
change	v.	stasis
action	v.	inaction
nature	v.	art
honesty	v.	deception
good	v.	evil

Not all characters fit this matrix. Lord Warburton, for example, is urbane and conscious of form, but he is admirable; Henrietta Stackpole, who is free and open, should learn to put a sock in it. Our Isabel represents the best of America.

to his side. She strikes up a friendship with Madame Merle, an old friend of the family. Ralph Touchett knows that his father plans to leave him the huge family fortune, but since he is also about to kick the bucket, he persuades his father to leave the money to Isabel. "If she has an easy income," he reasons, "she will never have to marry." Ironically, the money causes Isabel to lose her freedom.

After her uncle dies, Isabel and her aunt travel to Italy, where Madame Merle engineers a match between Isabel and Gilbert Osmond, a vintage lounge lizard. She marries the creep and he systematically tries to crush her joie de vivre. The guy's had practice: he has already destroyed the spirit of his daughter Pansy.

When Isabel hears that her cousin Ralph is dying, she wants to go to England to see him. Osmond puts his foot down; Isabel steps on it. In England, she tells the conveniently present Caspar Goodwood that she goofed and married the wrong man. He wants her to leave her husband, but she decides to stand by her man.

FREE TO BE YOU AND ME

Most novelists begin with a theme and set about creating a situation in which it can be played out. Henry, in contrast, began with a situation. Into this would go characters and then The Master would see where things went. He let the situations and the characters determine the end rather than shaping them to a preconceived finale.

In this novel we have a charming young girl who arrives in Europe but lacks the means to travel. Whatever

shall we do? In the timeless tradition of James's predecessor, Jane Austen, Isabel decides to find a man. She does
so, but it destroys her chance to develop freely to the
limits of her own ability. Notice that Henry himself
stayed single.

POINT OF VIEW . . . .

Henry is also noted for his contribution to the way stories are told. Before Henry, most of the fiction was written from the author's viewpoint. In Henry's novels, we
see the action unfold through the eyes of the central
character. Called the central intelligence, it enables
readers to react to the story as the character would.

A FEW OTHER NOVELS
BRIEFLY DISCUSSED . . .

THE AMERICAN

When Titans Clash: The New Man
in the Old World

Isabel Archer's male counterpart is Christopher Newman, another innocent, enthusiastic romantic. A self-
made millionaire, Newman travels to Paris to find culture
and companionship—of the female variety. He meets
Tom Tristram, an old friend, and tells him he is shopping for a spouse. The obliging Mrs. Tristram fixes Newman up with a widow, Madame Claire de Cintre, a
member of one of Europe's oldest aristocracies. She's a
looker but lacks moxie.

Newman calls on Madame de Cintre, her brother Valentin, and her sister-in-law, the Marquise de Bellegarde. Valentin and Newman hoist a few together and Newman announces his intentions. Although Valentin is shocked—how dare a nouveau riche American set his sights on the aristocracy?—he agrees to help. Soon after, Newman proposes to Claire. She is surprised and makes him agree to let her think about the matter for six months.

WHO'S WHO ☞

The American:
A LITERARY TOUT SHEET

Christopher Newman: The "new man" discovering the Old World. Great bod, good mind, tender feelings: a keeper.

Madame Claire de Cintre: Look but don't touch. Could be Galatea to Newman's Pygmalion: one kiss and marble becomes flesh.

Valentin de Bellegarde: Aristocrat with a high sense of honor and integrity, which unfortunately proves his doom when he is killed in a duel.

The Bellegardes: The Ice King and his Queen: the aristocracy at its worst. The "beautiful guards," the English translation of their frenchified name, of the old order.

After the statute of limitations is over, Newman renews his suit, and to everyone's astonishment, Madame de Cintre accepts. The Bellegardes throw a wingding to celebrate and everyone boogies the night away. Life is grand. Newman buys a new tux.

The next time Newman calls on Claire, he is astonished to learn that she has changed her mind; instead of marrying him, she is going to become a nun. He is sure that the family is behind her change of heart. Valentin tells Newman to see Mrs. Bread, the housekeeper, who has some information that would force the family to keep their word. Newman gets the goods on the Bellegardes, but rather than going through with the blackmail, throws the letter into the fire.

ALL'S WELL THAT ENDS WELL

Only curmudgeons were satisfied with the ending; everyone else howled long and loud. "They would have been an impossible couple," Henry explained his defense. And then we have the practical considerations. Where would they live—his bailiwick or hers? Can we see Claire punching cows on the range? Henry himself had serious second thoughts, because he substituted a happy ending when he dramatized the novel. Seven years after he published the novel, Henry tried to beat the issue to death. No wonder that, years later, he reversed himself in other parts of the novel. In a preface to the novel written near the end of his life, Henry believed that the Bellegardes would have been delighted to welcome Newman to the fold.

MONETARY GAIN
· ·
Henry started writing *The American* in 1875, planning
to issue it in nine installments in *The Atlantic Monthly*.
The editor was his good friend William Dean Howells,
the highly influential critic, editor, and novelist. The installments grew to twelve, but Henry made every dead-
line on time. For his labor, he received $150 per
installment. But then again, that's
when a dollar was really a dollar.

*William Dean Howells (1837–1920).
Friend and editor to James; proponent
of Realism (with a capital "R") in
literature; writer of novels, short stories,
plays, memoirs, and literary criticism.*

THE TURN OF THE SCREW:
WHO YOU GONNA CALL?

Chewing the fat with some friends one night, a man
named Douglas reads the manuscript left by his sister's
governess many years ago. Before he reads, Douglas explains that a handsome and rich bachelor had hired the
governess to assume total control for a young girl and
her brother. The governess, a sucker for a handsome
face, accepted the job at once.

The governess travels to the house, called Bly, where
she meets Mrs. Grose, a servant, and eight-year-old Flora.
The day before the boy, Miles, is due home, the govern-

ess gets a letter from the headmaster of his school—
Miles has been given the boot. The governess wonders
if Miles is a Bad Seed, but when he arrives, he's such a
cute ten-year-old that she sets aside her fears.

Soon after, the governess glimpses an unfamiliar man
in one of the towers of the mansion. She keeps the encounter to herself. A few days later, she sees him again,
but he vanishes. Mrs. Grose explains that it is Peter

WHO'S
WHO

The Turn of the Screw:
A LITERARY TOUT SHEET

The governess: Sexually repressed ghostbuster,
the youngest daughter of a country parson who
is definitely in over her head.

Mrs. Grose: As her name suggests, the housekeeper is the link to the real world.

Miles: Adorable ten-year-old boy who is either
an innocent pawn or the devil's spawn.

Flora: Beautiful eight-year-old girl who falls
from innocence to experience.

Peter Quint: The former servant and current
ghost.

Miss Jessel: Did the wild thing with Peter
Quint and came to a sorry end.

The uncle: Rich bachelor who prefers the
child-free life.

Quint, a former employee. Unfortunately for the governess's sanity, he's dead. Oooooohhh.

Then she sees a female ghost, whom Mrs. Grose identifies as the previous governess, Miss Jessel. Yes, also dead. The ghosts keep popping up, we presume, and the governess keeps hoping someone would invent Valium. The governess becomes convinced that the ghosts have corrupted the children. After coming face to face with Miss Jessel's ghost, our heroine decides it's time to write to the uncle.

One typically soggy English day, the governess confronts Flora and demands to know where Miss Jessel is hiding. The governess sees Miss Jessel on the other side of the lake, but the child and Mrs. Grose see nothing. Flora collapses and spikes a temperature. The next morning Mrs. Grose says that she believes there is a ghost, based on what Flora is mumbling in her delirium.

That night, Miles admits that he has taken the letter meant for his uncle. He also reveals that he had been telling his classmates about the family's otherworldly visitors. As they talk, the governess sees the ghost of Peter Quint at the window. In a battle for the boy's soul, the governess tries to shield him from the horror. Finally she points to the ghost, but Miles falls into her arms, dead.

LIKE A VIRGIN

On the surface, what we have is a neat little ghost story, delightfully terrifying. But you know those literary critics; never satisfied with anything. One such critic, Edmund Wilson, thinks that the governess has a Problem: a virgin spinster, she is so sexually repressed that she creates the ghosts herself. His case is good: no one else sees the apparitions and there is no objective proof that they exist. But also keep in mind that Wilson was writing in 1934 and was big on Freud. Hate to do this to you, but you have to read the story yourself to decide. Not to worry; it's among Henry's shortest and most accessible works.

Then we have the works of his Major Phase. *The Golden Bowl* is one of the "three poetic masterpieces" of his later period, as fellow novelist Graham Greene has called it. It is also his most controversial novel; critics have argued vociferously about the unusual plot, in which a terribly rich American and his daughter marry a pair of lovers. *The Ambassadors,* which James himself judged "the best all 'round" of his novels, and *The Wings of the Dove,* also from this period, are demanding novels because of their rich syntax, symbolic resonance, and metaphor.

SUMMARY

 Psychological realist of unsurpassed subtlety.

 Preserved a way of life most of us will never know, more's the pity.

 Wrote well in several genres, including lit. crit, novels, and short stories. His plays we don't talk about; you shouldn't know from them.

 Remained absolutely loyal to his craft.

 Infuses his work with a moral sense, a sense of decency and humanity.

CHAPTER 12

JOSEPH CONRAD

(1857–1924)

YOU MUST REMEMBER THIS

Conrad was one of the greatest English novelists and perhaps the finest prose stylist of them all. All his major characters grapple with an agonizing moral dilemma.

MOST FAMOUS FOR

Long novels, short novels, but always dense novels, including:

- ★ *Heart of Darkness* (1899)
- ★ *Lord Jim* (1900)
- ★ *Nostromo* (1904)
- ★ *The Secret Agent* (1906)
- ★ *Under Western Eyes* (1910)
- ★ *The Secret Sharer* (1912)

SHIP, AHOY

Conrad was born Józef Teodor Konrad Walecz Korzeniowski. He later shortened his moniker to "Conrad" because the original wouldn't fit on a dust jacket. His father was a poet, critic, and translator of Shakespeare, which undoubtedly influenced Conrad's choice of a career. As a small child, he was forced to leave Poland when his parents were sent into exile in Russia for their activities on behalf of Polish independence. It's possible that the borsch, Bolsheviks, and babushkas didn't agree with the Korzeniowskis, for they soon died, leaving their son in the care of his maternal uncle, Tadeusz Bobrowski. That's when Józef headed for adventure. At age fifteen, he amazed Uncle Tad by shipping out to sea. He refused to enter the naval academy in Pola where future officers were trained. Instead, it was a lowly sailor's life for him. After much discussion, in 1874 Józef was allowed to ship out on a French merchant ship to Martinique and the West Indies. In 1878, he signed on a British merchant ship and learned to speak

---

FAMOUS QUOTE . . . .
Conrad's most quoted line is "The Horror! The Horror!" from *Heart of Darkness*; it is Kurtz's acknowledgment of the darkness of the human soul. Francis Ford Coppola reworked *Heart of Darkness* around the Vietnam experience and called it *Apocalypse Now*. From that movie came another famous quote, "I love the smell of napalm in the morning."

English. Eight years later he became a naturalized British subject, and two years after that, received his first command position.

In 1889, Conrad returned to England from a long voyage, and obeying "a sudden and incomprehensible impulse," began to write his first novel, *Almayer's Folly*. Most people, when confronted by such an urge, go shopping or clean the garage instead, but not our pal Joey. A year later, acting almost as impulsively, he set the novel aside and secured the command of a small vessel headed for the upper Congo. He remained in Africa for several months, nearly dying of fever and dysentery, and returned to England svelte but depressed. The severe illness and horrifying conditions of Hell Year on the Congo permanently scarred his psyche. *Heart of Darkness* is his only-slightly fictionalized account of life among tsetse flies the size of stealth bombers.

In 1892, while serving as a first mate on a ship sailing from London to Australia, he bent the ear of a sympathetic or slow-moving passenger with the plot of *Almayer's Folly*. The passenger turned out to be John Galsworthy, who gave him both encouragement and connections.

Conrad settled in London and in 1896 married Jessie George, a typist sixteen years his junior. The marriage did not get off to an auspicious start: during the honeymoon the groom was acutely ill and spent most of his time shouting deliriously at his wife in Polish. Nevertheless, the marriage endured, producing two sons, Borys and John (named after Galsworthy). A career in low gear, overcooked British vegetables, and a growing family exacerbated Conrad's naturally saturnine disposition. In

JOHN GALSWORTHY

John Galsworthy (1867–1933) was a distinguished novelist and dramatist. His oeuvre concerns life among upper middle-class English families who favor watercress-and-butter sandwiches without the crusts. Eventually he zeroed in on the life and times of one such family, a tony bunch he called the *Forsytes*. Their collected adventures appear in a volume called *The Forsyte Saga*. For his efforts, Galsworthy received the 1932 Nobel Prize in literature. Today he is primarily known for having written enough to keep public television's *Masterpiece Theatre* busy for multiple seasons.

1894, Conrad finally completed *Almayer's Folly*. For his efforts he earned twenty pounds and mediocre reviews. But he had some aces up his sleeve: extraordinary talent, stunning determination, and influential friends. Aside from Galsworthy, his supporters included Edward Garnett, an editor; and writers Ford Madox Ford and Henry James. James, no mean draw with a pen himself, admired Conrad's writing so greatly that he always called him "Cher Maître" (that's "Dear Master" to you non-French-speakers). Conrad generously returned the favors that came his way: even before he was famous himself, he tried to help struggling writers, including the young American novelist Stephen Crane.

Despite his friends in publishing, Conrad's career did not go smoothly. His novels rarely made money, and he was often forced to set aside a book in mid-sentence to churn out short stories to make some quick change. His health was bad; he suffered from bouts of depression and gout; what's more, his foul temper became legendary. Nonetheless, he persevered with his craft until 1924, when he quietly slipped out of his chair and died.

Joseph Conrad, professional sailor, didn't much favor the genteel plots of his day: girl marries wrong boy, boy marries wrong girl, complications ensue, everyone jumps into a bog. Conrad went for blood and guts and sociopaths and heavy weapons. What can you expect from a Conrad plot? You're in for crime in the Congo, revolution in a South American banana republic, political terrorism in London, love in steaming seaports, murder in St. Petersburg, and cowardice on sinking ships. Not to mention a bloated Brando in the jungle of *Apocalypse Now*, acting out the part of Kurtz with guttural sangfroid.

Conrad's novels probe human nature and destiny. He helped usher in the creation of the modern psychological novel.

FORD MADOX FORD: HAVE YOU READ A FORD, LATELY?

Don't confuse Ford Madox Ford with Henry: the first drove a car; the second built them. Ford Madox Ford (1873–1939) was born with the less-redundant but harder to spell surname "Hueffer." In addition to changing his name, he wrote two novels with Joseph Conrad—*The Inheritors* (1901) and *Romance* (1903). On his own he produced a number of books, including *The Good Soldier, Some Do Not* (1924), *No More Parades* (1925), and *A Man Could Stand Up* (1926). Four of his novels were reissued posthumously as *Parade's End* (1950). He also wrote a biography of Conrad.

CONRAD TODAY

For many years Conrad was regarded as a writer of the sea, appreciated primarily for his exotic locales and diverting plots. In the last thirty years, however, he's been awarded a prime spot in the parking lot of English fiction. Now he's on the first tier with Jane Austen, George Eliot, Henry James, and D. H. Lawrence as a maker of "the great tradition" in English fiction. This is because critics and readers have looked beyond his exciting plots to see the moral symbolism and psychological complexity of his novels. Conrad tackled the Big Themes—the meaning of life, civilization, and heroism—and makes his readers apply these themes to their own lives.

ALWAYS A BRIDESMAID, NEVER A BRIDE

Among other writers of fiction, literary critics occupy a particular region in hell, for they are capable of making or breaking a novelist's reputation without ever having written fiction of their own. The authors they disparage no doubt place them right down there with film, theater, and art critics. Among Conrad scholars, the formidably talented biggies are Alfred Guerard, Leo Gurko, F. R. Leavis, Ian Watt, Daniel R. Schwarz, Morton D. Zabel, Dorothy Van Ghent, and Robert Penn Warren. Fortunately, they all give Conrad four stars.

HEART OF DARKNESS:
THE HORROR! THE HORROR!

As his vessel lies docked in London, Marlow tells his captive audience a tale of his extraordinary experience in ivory trade of the Congo. He arrived at the company's lower station and was appalled by the tragic conditions: natives worked to death and piles of rusting machinery. The chief accountant tells Marlow all about Kurtz, the legendary agent who ships out more ivory than all the other agents combined.

Soon after, Marlow treks inland two hundred miles to the company's main station. He then steams upriver, a journey of two months, and finally arrives at Kurtz's station. A Russian, Kurtz's disciple, explains that his master has become a god to the natives, even participating in their secret rites. The severed heads posted on stakes around Kurtz's hut are a subtle tip-off to the heady drama of these quaint customs. Kurtz may be a god, but these guys haven't exactly been learning their catechism.

That night Kurtz sneaks into a savage devil ceremony. Marlow goes after him and glimpses the unimaginable

WHO'S WHO ☞

Heart of Darkness:
A LITERARY TOUT SHEET

Marlow: Symbol redux: the good self, the moral man.

Kurtz: Came to the Congo to bring Civilization to the natives; ends up going native himself.

General Manager: The closest thing we get to a villain, the manager is responsible for all the cruelty, neglect, and waste of the operation.

degradation of the human soul. Kurtz explains his rise to power. He had traveled to the jungle to teach the natives and "civilize" them; instead, he was corrupted by the very evil he wished to conquer. Kurtz dies, crying, "The horror! The horror!" Marlow takes ill and is shipped home. There, he visits Kurtz's "intended," who holds her fella to be most noble and true. Marlow lies and tells the woman that Kurtz's last words were of her.

Marlow's trip up the Congo is a journey into the heart of human nature. The title symbolizes both the Congo and the darkness within us. Like *The Secret Sharer, Heart of Darkness* is an exploration of the primitive, subconscious aspects of even civilized souls. The novel's political message remains potent a century later: moved by greed and

Holy Communion in the midst of battle. A scene from Apocalypse Now *(American Zoetrope, 1979), writer/director/producer Francis Ford Coppola's updated take on* Heart of Darkness.

arrogance, people in power still try to bring "civilization" to "backward" races. Though, like Kurtz, they often begin in all sincerity, they do not fully understand their true motivation. The maniacal Kurtz seems to be at the center of the novel, much as Leggatt appears to be the crux of *The Secret Sharer*. But though Kurtz's role is flamboyant, the character of Marlow is in some ways more interesting, for it is with Marlow that the reader is likely to identify. Marlow (aka the reader) feels the tug of the untamed himself, and thus his contact with the wildman Kurtz obliges us to contemplate the vestigial savagery that lurks within ourselves.

LORD JIM: MARLOW'S THE NAME, HONOR THE GAME

Jim is an officer aboard the *Patna*, a rickety pilgrim ship ferrying eight hundred devout Asians to the holy lands. When the vessel seems about to sink, Jim, his captain, and two other officers abandon ship. But tough break: the *Patna* doesn't sink and Jim and his buddies are in deep trouble. Hauled before a court of inquiry, they are each interrogated about their behavior. The other crewmen go on the lam, leaving Jim alone to face conviction for having failed to fulfill his responsibilities as an officer of the ship. He is found guilty and deprived of his seaman's certificate; that is, his means of earning a living.

During the hearing, Jim meets Marlow, an older seaman. Later, Marlow gets Jim a number of jobs as a "water clerk," but Jim is forced to move on each time his identity as a former officer of the *Patna* is uncovered.

With the help of his friend Stein, Marlow finally gets Jim a position in Patusan, a remote Malay village. Redeeming his failed career, Jim becomes the village leader, bringing a chicken to every pot and a Land Rover to every garage. (Well, not really, but he does bring peace to the troubled land.) For his success, the natives call him "Tuan Jim"—Lord Jim. Feeling that he has made amends for his cowardice, Jim takes a significant other, Jewel, the beautiful stepdaughter of the evil Cornelius, Stein's new agent.

But paradise gained is soon paradise lost. "Gentleman Brown," a brigand of the old school, attacks Patusan. Anxious that his people be left in peace, Jim cuts a deal with Brown, but the pirate reneges and, in a violent ambush, kills many innocent extras. Among the victims is Dain Waris, the heir apparent to the throne of Patusan. The Patusans pin the blame on Jim, who bravely faces the mob and allows himself to be shot by Dain Waris's

IN LITERATURE AS IN LIFE . . .

Conrad drew many of his plots from his own experiences. *Lord Jim* is based on the story of the pilgrim ship *Jeddah,* which set out from Singapore in 1880 with 950 passengers bound for the holy lands. The ship suffered the same fate as the *Patna*: her officers deserted in much the same manner, and the resulting scandal was water-cooler talk around the Far East even before water coolers were invented. Conrad heard the story when he disembarked in Singapore in 1883, although he did not write the book for fifteen years.

WHO'S HO ☞

Lord Jim:
A LITERARY TOUT SHEET

Jim: A young, handsome Englishman who jumps ship faster than you can say "big-time leak." For his cowardice, Jim becomes an outcast and is forced to wander through the East like Moses through the desert.

Marlow: Although Jim won in the title category, Marlow is the moral center of the book. He's the older, honorable sea captain (often identified with Conrad) who represents idealism and honor.

Captain of the *Patna*: Prime candidate for Ultra Slim Fast, the skipper is a craven coward who flees rather than take the rap for his dereliction. Besides, he can barely fit into his pajamas.

Jewel: The name says it all; Jim's, er, love interest.

Gentleman Brown: Terror on the high seas; the pirate.

Dain Waris: Heir apparent to the throne of Patusan; killed in the end.

father, Doramin. Marlow concludes that Jim has made "an extraordinary success" of his life.

So what does it all mean? Call in the heavy guns: honor, heroism, greatness. Many critics see Jim as a Hero because he has fulfilled his Duty and Responsibility, thus earning Greatness. And indeed he has, but at an enormous personal cost—his life. Conrad is also concerned with nature's indifference, human failure, and human possibility. He conveys the psychological complexity of these issues through symbols and implication, and readers must judge for themselves the meaning of Jim's actions.

There is also the matter of Conrad's style. Metaphors, similes, personification abound, and they are pretty things. Here's a sample passage that has it all: "The sky over Patusan was blood red, immense, streaming like an open vein. An enormous sun nestled crimson amongst the treetops, and the forest below had a black and forbidding face." This skill with figurative language, imagery, and sentence style has earned Conrad accolades.

THE SECRET SHARER: THEY TALK ALIKE, THEY WALK ALIKE: YOU COULD LOSE YOUR MIND

An unnamed ship is anchored in the Gulf of Siam. The captain, also unnamed, is the new kid on the block. He's been the head weenie at the roast for two weeks now, but his crew sneer at his inexperience and lack respect for what abilities he has. He offers to take the last watch himself to give his men a full night's sleep.

Before the crew goes to bed, he sees another ship about two miles away. His second mate identifies the ship as the *Sephora.*

After everyone has been tucked in, the Captain discovers that the ship's rope ladder is still hanging over the side. As he pulls on the ladder, he discovers a swimmer attached. The swimmer introduces himself as "Leggatt" and explains that he is on the lam after murdering a fellow crew member aboard the *Sephora.* He is not really at fault, he claims: he accidentally strangled the mutinous dogsbody during a storm. Captain and castaway are about the same age and size. Despite the new arrival's confession, the Captain feels an instant kinship with this double and hides him in his cabin, at what the skipper imagines to be considerable risk to his own person.

When the *Sephora*'s skipper comes to search his ship for the escaped criminal, the captain thwarts his investigation and convinces the skipper that Leggatt has drowned, because he does not want Leggatt captured and brought to justice. The captain's ruse is successful, but his identification with Leggatt mounts. The captain decides to help his double escape to Koh-ring, a nearby island.

He gives Leggatt three gold coins and his own white hat to protect him from the burning tropical sun. His crew thinks he is crazy to bring the ship so close to land that the vessel is at risk of being wrecked. But the captain steers with such skill that he succeeds both in surreptitiously delivering his "secret sharer" to safety (Leggatt swims ashore from the moving ship) and earning the respect of the crew.

WHO'S
H
O

The Secret Sharer:
A LITERARY TOUT SHEET

The Captain: Still damp behind the ears, the unnamed Captain is a twenty-seven-year-old hunk who looks great in his jammies. (Actually, it seems that everyone in Conrad novels wears pajamas. One almost begins to wonder about the absence of lounge chairs and breakfast trays on Conrad's merchant ships.)

Leggatt: The captain's clone is the evil twin Skippy: the houseguest who nearly overstays his welcome.

The crew: Assorted whiskered, bandy-legged salts.

Recall that Conrad was a career sailor who lived by the rigid laws and pitiless traditions of the sea. To an officer who adhered to this code, killing a man under your command was a crime, no matter what his offense. The captain hides and protects Leggatt because, contrary to the code, he comes to identify with him in a visceral, irresistible way. Leggatt's brutal act causes the captain to realize that under such circumstances, he too could have lost control and murdered a man under his command. Through this realization, the young captain gains an understanding of the good and evil present in every human soul, and so achieves a kind of maturity he lacked when the voyage began. The captain has undergone a journey of self-exploration, self-recognition, and self-control. Since this is Conrad, the tale delivers a message that is somewhat gloomy: with self-awareness comes the knowledge that we are threatened most of all by our own capacity to commit evil acts. And just when you thought it was safe to go back into the water!

SUMMARY

Celebrated for his finely honed style, psychological complexity, and moral symbolism.

Probes our primitive, darker side: every Conrad character struggles with a moral dilemma (and for that matter, they all seem to wear gray pajamas).